THE ART AND SCIENCE OF

Handwriting

ROSEMARY SASSOON

The Burne
by Ben Jonson

It is not easy for me to find samples of my early lettering. Each job of work was completed and sent to the client. There were none of the exhibition pieces that are so popular today and I did not bother to have anything photographed. The three examples shown here are from rough copies of commissions. They had been stored away in some safe place, and must have survived several moves of house over the years.

This golf club notice dates back to 1950. The heading is from a poem lettered in the early 1980s as a memorial for a child who died young. One of the key lines of the poem is 'A lillee of a day is fairer farre in May'.

Knole Park
Ladies' Golf Club
Hole In One
Name   Hole Length Date

THE ART AND SCIENCE OF

Handwriting

ROSEMARY SASSOON

intellect

OXFORD, ENGLAND

First published in Great Britain in 1993 by
Intellect Books
Suite 2, 108/110 London Road, Oxford OX3 9AW

Consulting editor: Masoud Yazdani
Copy editor: Wendy Momen
Index: Roy Davies

Designed by Pardoe Blacker Publishing Limited
Shawlands Court, Newchapel Road, Lingfield, Surrey

British Library Cataloguing in Publication data

Sassoon, Rosemary
Art and Science of Handwriting
I. Title
372.6

ISBN 1-871516-33-1

Printed and bound in Great Britain by Bath Press, Bath

Contents

Acknowledgements

I owe a great deal to the many people in so many fields who have taught me their disciplines, entrusted me with their patients and helped me to formulate my ideas in a scientific setting. First to Alan Wing who plucked me from my lettering studies, and while generously pretending that he needed my knowledge of letterforms, helped me far more than I was ever able to help him. At the same time Ian Nimmo-Smith introduced me to computers and dealt with my statistical shortcomings. While Briem urged and bullied me into deeper letterform and computer studies, and taught me effective techniques of presenting my work, Michael Twyman squeezed me into a more consistent and logical frame of thought. I owe a lot to friends in IGS who treated me gently in my early presentations and put up with my questions even when I was challenging some of their ideas, and of course to my husband John for his wise counsel, and unfailing support. I owe debts to my various editors who have guided me and taught me the craft of writing and in this present enterprise I thank my brave editor Masoud Yazdani, who commissioned this and its companion, *Computers and Typography* (Intellect 1993).

Preface

This collection of papers and articles has provided me with a valuable opportunity to gather together a decade's work on handwriting and to see it all in perspective. It gives me a chance to trace the sequence of events and the gradual evolution of my theories as one study after another opened up aspects of handwriting that had not previously been investigated.

The details of the techniques that had to be evolved in order to measure the various elements of writing and writing posture will be reported in the following chapters. What is not so easy to reveal are the subtle alterations in direction as findings brought me increasing confidence to experiment further and further away from the conventional attitudes to letters and other matters.

Apart from the extensive formal research project that was already in action, all through the 80s my policy was to see and treat as many people with handwriting problems as possible. I offered my services to a wide variety of hospitals and schools, letting it be known at in-service sessions that I would be willing to see those with serious problems free of charge, at any time. In this way I was exposed to a fortuitous mixture of able-bodied children and adults and those with severe medical problems. This gave me a wider perspective than specialist teachers or therapists are usually able to gather in their professional lives. With the ever more perplexing problems, it was the patients themselves, both children and adults, who taught me much of what I now know. With educational problems it was often easier to say what was wrong rather than what was right. Some answers, however, were to be found by observing the effects of a variety of different models and methods in countries worldwide with vastly different ideas. It is necessary to study other writing systems too, both ancient and modern. The real truths are not to be found in one writing system alone.

As I dug deeper, usually working on field studies so that I could concentrate on the realities of handwriting, it became clear to me that older research, not always even reported in this country, had sometimes more to offer than many modern studies. The writing masters of the fifteenth century understood the relationship between the hand, the pen and the resulting trace. Some doctors in the last century wrote more sensibly about the problems of writer's cramp than many specialists do today, and the work of the one man who could support my own theories about penhold had not been translated into English and was virtually unknown. In education, Montessori, almost a century ago, understood precisely the involvement of the motor memory in the training of young children, whereas too much educational research today tries to justify some particular model or prescribe some hypothetical norm without any understanding of the complexity of the act. When it came to judging handwriting legibility, the important typographic research of the 1930s that explains so clearly the many complex factors that influence the legibility of letterforms was ignored, and still is for that matter.

I have given ten years to handwriting research and inevitably have not had the time nor the facilities to go as deeply as I would have liked into many areas. It is against that background that these papers are presented. In many cases the papers explain that the work reported is exploratory. They offer methods and encourage readers to replicate the studies in different countries and with different groups of writers. Several published articles are included in this book. They depend on research findings as well as on observations undertaken in many different circumstances, in different parts of the world, for the advice and conclusions that they present.

At the same time, I have been busy writing a series of books aimed at teachers and therapists. *The Practical Guide to Children's Handwriting* (Thames and Hudson 1983), *Teach Yourself Handwriting* (Hodder and Stoughton 1984), *Helping your Handwriting (*Nelson 1986, new edition OUP 1994) and a pair published by Stanley Thornes in 1990 entitled *Handwriting: The Way to Teach it*, and *Handwriting: A New Perspective,* all followed each other in quick succession. It might have been prudent to wait for proof of every statement that I needed to make, but long ago I began to doubt whether statistical evidence was either possible or desirable in many areas of handwriting. The intensely personal nature of the act of writing defies such definition. Whether it is in letterforms, writing implements or details of writing posture, it is the variability of the findings that are important in that they point to the need to consider the writer as well as the reader. The task needs to be considered in relation to the level and speed of writing, and we need to question the causes of all such variability and learn from it rather than to confine the child, or adult for that matter, in an inflexible and often arbitrarily selected set of rules. As I look back on these published books, there may be a few omissions in the earlier ones, but the philosophy is the same.

This decade of research and practical work has taught me many things that are not easily put into words. For instance, many people ask me how I associate various characteristics of handwriting to the writer. It is certainly not in the way of graphologists, who usually work from previously written examples. They may apply a specific set of rules to assist in their analysis, then make inferences about the characteristic disposition of the writer.

It is not as document examiners, who frequently have two previously written documents to compare. They use acute observational powers and other sets of rules to justify an impartial decision in court.

My instincts and judgements have been formed through a different set of circumstances. I have almost always had the writer in front of me. In this way the act of writing and the written trace can be observed at the same time. General body language can be taken into consideration as well as the alterations in writing strategies as the writers relax. It is inevitable, over so many cases, that there arises a pattern of characteristics related to certain elements of handwriting. Whatever I may suspect from my initial observations is used as a guide to further questioning. This helps me to understand and assist individuals to find new strategies and eventually a handwriting tailored to their specific needs.

Part 1

explains how I came to handwriting research from a background of letterforms and design. It then concentrates on my recent research projects. Some of the papers included in this book were published previously in different countries and some translated into other languages. Together at last, they can be judged as a body of work spanning a decade in my chosen field. Moreover, in each case, the formal paper is expanded to trace, through extended discussion, the implications of my research and to show how the findings influenced the progress and direction of my investigations.

CHAPTER 1

An Introduction to Letterforms

The title of this book is most appropriate, as it describes the two halves of my life in letterforms – the artistic and the scientific. Without the first, the second could not have come about. The discipline of letterforms is not easily understood by the majority of the populace who take letters, whether written or printed, very much for granted. It is never simple to explain the influences and perhaps coincidences that guide one to a lifetime's interest in a particular subject, but for me at least the timing is clear. I began to be fascinated by letterforms at the age of thirteen. My art teacher, as all others at that time, had been trained in lettering. At art school a happy chance brought an excellent lettering master and pretty rotten ones in the other subjects that might have seduced me from letterforms.

Things began to become more serious when I left art school and had the opportunity to study for several years, albeit part-time, with a master scribe. The training I had then differed little from that of a medieval scribe. At that particular moment, just after the war, there were many books of remembrance to produce, and few skilled enough to do so. We therefore had, just like scribes centuries before, to be able to sublimate any features of our own personalities that might appear in our letterforms to produce letters that were exact replicas of our masters'. This is no mean effort, and its influence was to remain with me for many years and eventually to colour my attitudes to following models whether in formal lettering or handwriting.

These words came from an exercise written in 1949. When we joined MC Oliver's class we were given a large reed pen and a bottle of home-brewed brown ink. Then we were retrained to make our letterforms as close as possible to those of our master's.

something rich

Our training might sound restrictive; maybe it was in some ways, but not in others. We were immersed in the history of writing. We

were not confined all the time to the pen, but encouraged to draw
and engrave letters. My first (and, until very recently, my only)
effort to design a typeface dates back to when I was eighteen.

What did this training contribute when it was necessary to
expand my field of activities? It meant that I knew letters, not only
from the visual 'outside' but from the inside. A scribe can look at a
letter and see as well as feel how it was written – where it starts
and which way it proceeds, where the pressures are and above all
whether the writer was tense or relaxed. When it was necessary,
for economic reasons, to go out of this somewhat sheltered
environment, it was to commercial lettering that I went. Again it
was a good moment, before the term 'graphic designer' had been
coined, or stick-on letters had been invented. In our studio we still
did everything by hand. Spacing was even more vital in drawn
lettering than it had been in pen-lettering. Printing techniques had
to be assimilated and a new set of priorities arose – most useful
ones too. It was a matter of pride, not the opposite, to conform to
a brief. Those were the early days of packaging and very early days
of advertising. You never knew what you would have to design
next. The inventiveness that we were encouraged to develop
during those years have stood me in good stead ever since.

You may think that all this has little to do with research into
handwriting, but I disagree. When people ask me how I can see so
much in a few moments in a handwriting example or posture –
whether in an English school or a Chinese one, a hospital or the
local bank – I assure them it did not come easily and it is not
magic. When I make a plea for interdisciplinary cooperation, it is
because I know only too well how little the discipline of
letterforms is understood. It is a lengthy study and only too seldom
undertaken thoroughly.

So what happened next? Eventually I decided to return to my
original specialty, lettering. By then, in the 70s, it had suffered a
metamorphosis. It had even changed names and was now known
as 'calligraphy'. In some sense it had lost its purpose and its soul,
because there was little real work left. What had for centuries been
a vital craft had become almost entirely a leisure activity. There
was a need for teachers of calligraphy – but I was not, and still am
not, a teacher by nature or training. The few scribes left had
preserved their craft as a lucrative and elitist activity, but what

These two monograms
illustrate the change in
my attitudes to letters
over the years. The first,
written in about 1951, is
tightly designed, whereas
the second, some thirty
years later, is freely
written.

interested me most was to evolve techniques so that ordinary people could learn. I refused the pleas of various art schools and started work in adult education. It was obvious that an easier method was needed for the general public than the one that I learned by, and is still widely used – give the student an alphabet to copy and let them get on with it.

An analytical approach to teaching beginners a new alphabet by separating the letters into stroke-related sequences. Reproduced from *The Practical Guide to Calligraphy*, Thames and Hudson (1982).

i l j m n r h u

Practise these letters first to get an even degree of compression

o c e a g b d p q

When round letters are compressed their sides are flattened

v w x y z s k ft

The diagonal stroke is at a steeper angle when letters are compressed

I was perfectly honest with my many students – they were involved in a research project. It made matters more interesting for everyone and it was not long before a systematic method evolved that brought considerable advances for beginners. First we dealt with purely practical matters: how to set up a slanting working board, with a resilient surface, and a method of leaving the paper free to move as the writer progressed along the line or down the page. Then the tool – a double pencil to begin with – and how to hold it. That short session ensured that everyone could sit and work in comfort. Patterns dealt with the problem of consistent pencil-angle, then letters were simplified and divided into stroke related sequences. The details of the terminals of letters were explained and practised before the pupils were let loose on the Foundational model. The letters of the model were taught in the same stroke related sequences, not the jumble of movements involved in alphabetical order. This method was put forward in my first book, *The Practical Guide to Calligraphy* (Thames and Hudson 1982). There was much to learn from observing this method. Even within such formalised exercises, the influence of the students' personal handwriting was evident. Some beginners could manage straight strokes while others slanted their letters however hard they concentrated. The same problems arose with letter proportions. Some students could reproduce with ease the round 'o's of the Foundational model, but many of them consistently produced a much more condensed version, more in line with their handwritten proportions. Furthermore many students found it difficult to perceive these alterations in the slant and proportions of letters as well as to produce them when they differed from their own previous perception or production of the forms.

Calligraphic patterns designed as place mats for the John Lewis Partnership.

Nonetheless, by being strict and methodical, and by developing self-criticism within the logical taught sequences, it was possible to get absolute beginners quite successfully on their way in one whole day-school (or two to three evening classes). It was much more difficult to deal with anyone who had previously experimented by themselves. There were clues as to why this should be, even then, offered by several primary schoolteachers who joined the early classes. They equated their new learning situation (new tool, new pencil hold, new movement of letters) with that of a five-year-old learning to write. It was not until I was lecturing about all this to a multi-disciplinary group of people interested in letterforms at the University of Reading that a more scientific answer was forthcoming. I had shown my examples to a rather doubting audience of specialists, who, after all, were most of them experts in one or other aspects of letterforms. They would have had very little understanding of unskilled adult education students and their first faltering steps towards lettering. In the audience, however, was an applied psychologist, Dr Alan Wing. He was involved in forensic and motor studies, both of which required a certain knowledge of letterforms. He approached me enthusiastically and volunteered that what I had been doing demonstrated the practical consequences of motor-training; in effect, the practical equivalent of his theoretical research. An invitation to work further with him was a turning point in my perception of the written trace.

In addition, shortly after this meeting, I was approached by my local education authority in Kent, to look into handwriting problems. Before accepting the invitation I spent some time visiting schools. I already knew the problems that arose from the insensitive and often inexpert imposition of idiosyncratic handwriting models. My own children and their peers had suffered from this during their schooling. It was through my 'letterer's' eyes, however, that I observed the contorted postures of the school children, and the way that neither they or their teachers had an understanding of the importance of the correct movement of letters. What I wrote for my first lecture in the late 1970s is still valid. I learned more detail through my research, I gained more confidence once I had the statistics to back my statements; but most of what I said then, and still say, is to me commonsense, based on the training and feel for letters that is natural to a scribe.

I continued teaching lettering for a few more years and developed a second teaching method for introducing beginners to letterforms – through the consistency of their own personal trace. This method was detailed in *The Practical Guide to Lettering* (Thames and Hudson 1985). Handwriting research, and handwriting problems, became a much higher priority in my life. I handed over my teaching and any subsequent lettering commissions to the most promising of my students and, with few backward glances, it was towards the scientific study of writing that I progressively gravitated.

My training and experience as a scribe had already convinced me that any study of the written trace should not be divorced from the act of writing. My early work on handwriting was influenced and informed by an extensive project that I set up to observe and analyse the act of writing and the written trace in relation to each other. These enquiries led me to certain conclusions and ever more deeply into the subject. With a background in letterforms, and help and encouragement from colleagues in other disciplines, the field was constantly expanded. Collaboration in psychological research led to more research into the medical aspects of handwriting problems, but at every turn I was confronted by the lack of informed research to back the views that were formulating. Educational research was in every way unsatisfactory. Physiological studies did not consider the features of the hand, for instance, that were relevant to handwriting, and only forensic research or paleographic studies seemed to look at letterforms in the scientific and non-stylistic way that was needed to proceed.

There are still a few investigations in the pipeline. The many examples gathered in my original survey could be analysed for years to come. Hundreds of photographs of posture and penholds could be tabulated in various ways. The children's signatures deserve much deeper analysis too, but other fields are opening up. My own work is diversifying, first into the area of second alphabet – or more accurately, second writing system – acquisition and then into computer-generated letterforms.

The area where letters for reading and letters for writing interact, whether in first or second language, is tempting too. There is far too little understanding of the effects of letterforms on children, whether for writing or for reading, whether computer-generated or handwritten. If I were to sum up my feelings in that area, it would be to say this: if you want to know what letters are easiest for anyone to read, anyone from a five-year-old upwards would probably be able to tell you, if given a suitable choice of examples, but do not expect the same answer from everyone. When it comes to letters for writing, it is school leavers who should be consulted. They can tell you whether the model that they were taught provided them with an adequate handwriting for life – and I am afraid that very few would answer in the affirmative.

CHAPTER 2

The Hand that Writes

Introduction

The decade that I devoted to handwriting research may prove important in a way that was impossible to forsee at the outset. It may well be the last time that such detailed observations are possible in a pre-computer age. There have been great changes in education in the last few years. In 1980 few schools had computers for general use in infant classes. There was, as yet, no alternative to pencil and paper. Yet the teaching of handwriting was given a low priority. This action (or inaction) was fuelled by the 60s generation of teachers and theorists who believed such teaching to be repressive. As the years passed the situation was worsened by the retirement of the few stalwarts who resolutely maintained their belief in the teaching of the 'three Rs'.

The impetus to my research was provided by the obvious difficulties that pupils of all ages seemed to find in the task of writing. I set out to observe, analyse and diagnose in order to alleviate such problems. Inevitably this led to suggestions as to how strategies and letterforms could be developed to help our children to acquire a handwriting that would work for them into the twenty-first century. This was at a time when many people began to say that handwriting was dead. This is not the first time that this chorus had been heard. When Gutenberg invented moveable type, and again when the typewriter was invented, the same refrain was repeated. All that happened then was that the usage of handwriting altered. That certainly deserves consideration today. Many of the written tasks demanded of our best students exceed the capacity of their hands.

It is the hand that writes and the inextricable involvement between the hand and the written trace, that occupy much of this book. The analysis of penhold was the first paper that was published containing some of the findings of my research project. Inevitably it had to conform to the requirements of an academic publication, and that format does not always permit the more general observations to appear. I am grateful for this opportunity to enlarge on the more formal statistical presentation, both with an introduction and further discussion at the end of this chapter.

A search failed to reveal any previous publications that had tackled this relationship between the hand and the trace in a meaningful way. Just as I was beginning my project I submitted a poster paper, and attended a NATO conference on the Acquisition of Graphic Skills, at the University of Keele, in Staffordshire. To my astonishment, considering the title of the conference, there was only one paper other than my own on handwriting. Even those engaged in longitudinal developmental studies did not seem to have considered the written trace worthy of inclusion – children's scribbles or drawings, yes, but not letters or the acquisition of handwriting.

A conference that same summer (1982) at the University of Nijmegen, in the Netherlands, indicated where the focus of handwriting research lay. It was in motor studies, and as such most of the serious research was being conducted as laboratory studies. While understanding the importance of such studies to the furthering of scientific knowledge – of the motor system in particular – it seemed to me that computer-linked techniques do not and cannot record the unconscious act of writing in a meaningful way. I felt that myself when I was asked to be a control subject for some on-line experiments that were being carried out in the Cambridge unit at the time. The whole procedure felt artificial to me, though I would obviously be termed an informed subject. The tool and the position of the pad induced an unfamiliar writing posture, and the whole atmosphere of being carefully observed produced a written example that was not in the least representative of my ordinary handwriting.

It seemed vital that an investigation into the task of writing should be undertaken in realistic surroundings. I also wanted to test different levels of handwriting – writing at ordinary speed and less conscious writing, at scribbling speed. All my testing techniques were designed to relax my subjects so as to obtain a natural written example and pictures of each individual's normal writing posture.

Part of my idea was to demonstrate that, with quite simple techniques, it was possible to measure quite complicated acts, and to reach valid conclusions from such findings. At that time there were no guidelines for informally testing or photographing to produce valid conclusions. Furthermore, there were no sensible methods at all to analyse the written trace in the way that it was obviously necessary. The methods of testing, the written tasks and the analyses all had to be novel. It was a miracle that it all turned out with so few errors, as there was little time for pilot schemes and no funding, only a strange urgency that drove me to attack this mountainous task. So much time and money is spent, especially in education, on fairly useless work. With so many pupils in trouble, their cause deserved immediate attention.

This paper was presented at the Second Conference of the International Graphonomics Society in Hong Kong in 1985. It was first published as Sassoon R, Wing AM and Nimmo-Smith I (1986) An Analysis of Children's Penholds in *Graphonomics, Contemporary Research in Handwriting*, eds Kao, van Galen and Hoosain, pp. 93-106. It is reproduced here by kind permission of North Holland Amsterdam, and my co-authors. Both of these generous friends, from the Medical Research Council Applied Psychology Unit, had given me a great deal of help from the start of my project and my data base remains with them in Cambridge.

Acknowledgements
1. Presentation of this paper was made possible by a British Council Grant to RS.
2. We are grateful to the children, teachers and Education Committee of Kent County Council for assistance in undertaking this study.

AN ANALYSIS OF CHILDREN'S PENHOLDS

Historical background

Writing masters have long stressed the connection between the way the writing implement is held and the resulting strokes of the pen. Thus, for example, Lucas (1571) described four errors 'particularly damaging to anyone who embodies them in his penhold.' These errors related to the positioning of the arm and to the use of the fingers and thumb in supporting and moving the pen. We may presume the damage referred to by Lucas involved factors such as quality of line and consistency of letterform.

As letterform models and writing tools changed so did penholds. Writing masters gave detailed descriptions of both finger and hand positions to ensure optimum penhold to achieve desired letterforms with specific writing implements. For example, Mercator (1540), using a square-cut quill to achieve italic letterforms (chancery script), advised (see Figure 1) a penhold with the hand on edge, thumb and finger (interphalangeal) joints extended and any weight of the hand not taken by the elbow 'supported only on the little finger, with the least possible pressure, thereby enabling the hand to move readily in any direction.' This description suggests writing was accomplished largely by movement of the whole hand rather than by finger movement. Gordon (undated, nineteenth century) gives rather different instructions for writing copperplate letterforms using a flexible, fine-pointed metal nib. He observed that 'ragged edges will be produced if the hand is allowed to rest on the side', and suggested

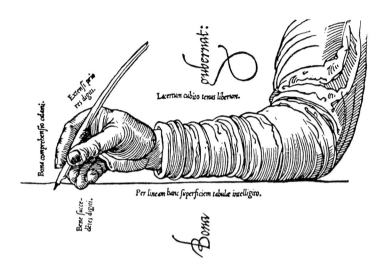

Figure 1
Penhold advocated by
Mercator (1540).

'the wrist should be kept nearly flat'. Instead of an extended thumb
he stated it should be flexed with 'the nail in fact almost, or quite,
touching the pen, with the thumb as much under the pen as
possible'. Letter formation was the result of thumb and finger
action.

In Britain there is at present no uniform policy for teaching
handwriting in schools. Letterform models in use range from italic
to cursives derived from copperplate. Modern writing implements
used in schools often differ considerably from the pens for which
the models were originally designed. Unlike nibbed pens, for
example, the modern ball-point pen, produces a written trace of
uniform line thickness, with little constraint on direction of
movement of the pen point. However, the ball-point does require
the pen to be held relatively upright. There is, in general, less
emphasis on handwriting appearance, provided the writing is
legible. Speed has become an important factor. If, as seems
reasonable, writing is a product of letterforms, writing implement
and penhold, the current lack of educational emphasis on the
process of writing may be expected to be of some consequence.

Working in an educational context, one of us (RS) has observed
a variety of penholds used by children when writing. Even casual
observation reveals that some of these penholds deviate quite
markedly from what is usually termed the dynamic tripod (e.g.

Figure 2
Details of penhold from
Gordon (undated
nineteenth century).

'The thumb should be
so bent that the upper
part is as as nearly as
possible at right angles
with the lower part.'

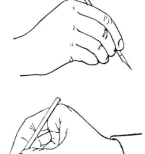

'The pencil should be
held by the right side of
the tip of the thumb,
the nail in fact almost,or
quite touching the
pencil, with the thumb
as much under the
pencil as possible.'

Elliott and Connolly 1984) where the pen is supported by the tips of the thumb, index and middle finger plus the web between the thumb and index finger. Does deviation from the dynamic tripod have an effect on the process of writing? Is the dynamic tripod, so favoured by teachers, the most efficient for all children? Is it perhaps more appropriate to the fountain pen than to the ball-point pen since the latter requires the pen barrel to be held more upright? However, before questioning the various penholds in these terms information is needed about the range of penholds currently employed by schoolchildren.

Classification of penholds

Although prescriptions for how to hold a pen may be found in the numerous books on handwriting instructions, we know of only one published study of penholds actually used by schoolchildren. In a survey of Australian children aged between 6 and 14 years, Ziviani (1983) recorded the presence or absence of four aspects of penhold based on the presence or absence of four features. The features were: flexed proximal interphalangeal joint of the index finger, pronated forearm, more than thumb and finger on the pen barrel, opposed thumb and finger. Ziviani claimed that her data revealed clear developmental trends in the nature of the penhold. In particular she stated that the proximal interphalangeal joint of the index finger was more likely to be strongly flexed in younger children and that they were more likely to pronate the forearm. Unfortunately, Ziviani's presentation of the proportion of children displaying a given feature was unadjusted for their age distribution so that the claimed age-related changes in grip must be treated with caution.

In the present paper we report a study of changes in penhold as a function of age in English schoolchildren between the ages of 7 and 16 years. Penholds are described in more detail than in the Ziviani study using a refinement of Jacobson and Sperling's (1976) approach to classifying hand-grips used in holding a variety of objects. As an index of changes in writing ability, we present data on writing speed and relate it to penhold.

Our classification scheme is summarised in Table 1 overleaf.

Table 1 Penhold classification summary

Feature	Values	
DIGITS		
Contact with pen	1: On barrel	2: Not on (or below, if finger)
Position on pen	1: Side	2: Top
	3: Half over	4: Right over
Proximity to pen tip	1: Nearest	2: Equal nearest
	3: Second	4: Equal second
	5: Third	6: Fourth
Shape of digit	1: Ext; ext.	2: Hypext; flex
(distal; proximal)	3: Flex; flex	4: Ext; flex
	5: Tucked in	

Feature	Values	
HAND		
Rotation	1: Slightly flattened	2: On edge
UPPER BODY		
Upper body posture	1: Upright	2: Body left; head right
	3: Bent left	4: Bent over top
	5: Bent right	6: Sits sideways
PAPER		
Orientation (re shoulder line)	1: Anticlockwise	2: Square
	3: Clockwise	
Position (re body midline)	1: Left	2: Centre
	3: Right	

Each of the five digits is first classed as to whether it touches the side or top of the pen barrel or if it is below or not in contact with the pen. Provided the digit is touching, the next three descriptors are scored. The second descriptor indicates where on the pen the digit makes contact. Defining top of the pen as the uppermost surface, the possible values for this descriptor are touching side, touching top, half-over the top (touching side and top), right-over (touching top and two sides). A third descriptor is relative proximity of the tip of the digit to the pen tip and this is

Figure 3
Penhold examples (redrawn by Pat Savage from original photographs) showing digit position on pen:

1

2

3

4

determined as nearest, equal nearest, second nearest, second equal, third and fourth.

A fourth descriptor for each digit refers to the angle of the interphalangeal joints. The first category is for the distal and proximal interphalangeal joints extended so that the three phalanges lie roughly in a straight line. If the distal interphalangeal joint is hyperextended so that the joint appears to be bent the wrong way (and this implies flexion of the more proximal interphalangeal joint), the second category is scored. A third category is for distal and proximal joints both flexed. A fourth category is distal extended, proximal flexed. The final category observed is for cases in which the digit is tightly 'curled up'. Some penholds, redrawn from photographs, are shown in Figures 3. They illustrate:

(1) Thumb and index both on side
(2) Thumb and index both on top
(3) Thumb half over
(4) Thumb right over

Postural description

While the focus of the present paper is on the description of penhold, the posture of the writer, including factors such as arm position, wrist angle, paper position, must also have an influence on writing. As a preliminary to further work we have therefore observed whether the forearm is pronated such that the hand appears either somewhat flattened or on edge. We note the angle of the wrist. Upper body posture is described in terms of any tendency to lean the head or body one way or the other with respect to the vertical. Also classified is the position of the paper in relation to the midline of the body (centred, left, right) and its orientation.

The survey

Subjects

The handwriting of children from three age group was sampled. The first group comprised 91 children (average age 7y 6m, SD 4m; 17 left-handed for writing) in their first year (following two years of primary education) at five state and one private junior schools in

Kent. All had mastered the use of at least pencils and ball-point pens in printing all the letters of the alphabet. With the exception of the private school children, they had not received class instruction in joining letters. The second group comprised 100 nine year-olds (average age 9y 6m, SD 4m; 10 left-handed for writing) in the third form of the same junior schools as the first group. They had all received some instruction in joining letters. However, handwriting instruction at two of the schools was based on italic model with little emphasis on joining letters. The other four schools taught cursive writing from different models. The third group of 103 children (average age 15y 8m, SD 3m; 16 left-handed for writing) were in their fourth year (the last year of compulsory schooling) in two separate secondary schools in the same geographic area as the first two groups. There was no class instruction of handwriting in the secondary schools.

Assessment procedure
Each child was tested individually by the first author (RS) in a session lasting 10 to 15 minutes. The child was seated at a school table with a horizontal surface. A black ball-point was supplied for writing. The paper used was wide (8mm)-ruled A4 which the child was allowed to position at a comfortable orientation. After writing his or her name, the child wrote out three different sentences presented on typed cards. The time taken to write each sentence was noted. To reduce unreliability in timing due to hesitations associated with spelling uncertainties, etc., practice was given with the first two sentences by having the children write them out once (fifteen-year-olds) or twice (seven- and nine-year-olds) before timing them. This was not necessary for the last sentence, which was based on a familiar nursery rhyme. The first two sentences were to be written at normal speed (i.e. without specific speed instructions), the third as rapidly as possible. Two sets of sentences were used: one set (lengths 8, 9 and 7 words) for the seven- and nine-year-olds; the other set (lengths 9, 13 and 8 words) for the secondary school children).

While the child was writing, usually during the second sentence, at least two photographs were taken from a point above and slightly in front of the child. These were used later to classify the nature of the penhold.

Figure 4
Penhold examples
showing a variety of
digit shapes

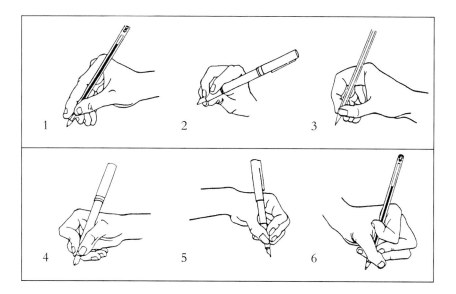

Figure 4
Penhold examples
showing a variety of
digit shapes

Top line:
(1) Thumb and index finger both ext; ext.
(2) Thumb hyperext; flex
(3) Index finger flex; flex

Bottom line:
(4) Index finger hyperext; flex
(5) Index finger ext; flex
(6) Index finger curled up

Results

The model category

The results of the classification of penhold are presented for the most part in terms of the modal category for each feature. The modal category is the most frequently occurring category of a mutually exclusive set of alternatives. Thus for example, Table 2 shows the frequencies of occurrence of the different categories of upper body posture. The modal category over all children is seen from the last column to be upright, and this also happens to be true of the different subgroups of children except for the left-handed nine-year-olds.

Table 2 Frequencies of occurrence of different upper body postures

Preferred hand:	Right			Left			
Age:	7	9	15	7	9	15	
POSTURE							
Upright	41	51	68	11	2	13	186
B Left; H Right	1	4	0	0	0	0	5
Bent left	28	26	8	0	0	0	62
Overtop	4	1	7	0	3	1	16
Bent right	0	2	4	6	5	2	19
Sideways	0	6	0	0	0	0	6
	74	90	87	17	10	16	294

Table 3 documents paper orientation and position. In this case the modal categories are different for right- and left-handers. Right-handers most often place the paper to the right, rotated anticlockwise whereas left-handers tend to place it centrally or to the left, rotated clockwise. Careful inspection shows the difference between left- and right-handers sharpens with age. This age by handedness interaction is statistically significant ($X^2(5)=24.1, p<01$).

The proportion of children with the hand on edge decreases with age from 33%, 25%, 14% for seven-, nine- and fifteen-year-olds.

Penholds described
We now turn to a summary of the modal features of the children's penholds. These are presented in Table 4 as percentages separately for each age group. The modal value for each feature was in all cases constant across age. Of particular interest are two findings that go against the typical pictures in handwriting manuals of the ideal penhold. The table shows that, in the majority of cases, the thumb rather than the index finger is closest to the tip of the pen and that there is usually hyperextensions at the distal interphalangeal joint of the index finger.

Table 3 Frequencies of occurrence of different paper positions and orientations

Preferred hand:	Right			Left			
Age:	7	9	15	7	9	15	
POSITION							
1 Left	1	0	6	8	4	8	27
2 Centre	29	15	6	8	6	7	71
3 Right	44	75	75	1	0	1	196
ORIENTATION							
1 AntiCW	35	78	83	0	2	2	200
2 Square	38	12	4	9	2	1	66
3 CW	1	0	0	8	6	13	28

Table 4 Modal penhold feature values and percentage of children at each age exhibiting modal value

Feature	Modal value	Age group		
		7	9	15
THUMB				
Contact	1: On barrel	100	100	100
Position	1: Side	55	61	61
Proximity	1: Leading	67	66	62
Shape	3: Flex; flex	86	92	89
INDEX FINGER				
Contact	1: On barrel	100	100	100
Position	1: Side	81	78	67
Proximity	3: Second	35	33	31
Shape	2: Hypext; flex	64	62	62

MIDDLE FINGER
Contact   2: Below/off   71   73   85

RING FINGER
Contact   2: Below/off   99   98   98

LITTLE FINGER
Contact   2: Below/off   100   100   100

It can be seen that, in general, the proportion of children in each age group using the modal feature is also very consistent. There are two notable exceptions. The first is that there is a reduction with age in the proportion of children positioning the index finger on the side of the pen; the contrast between the 7 and 9 year olds and the 15 year olds is statistically significant, ($X^2(1) = 5.6$, p<.05). The second change with age is the decreasing in frequency with which the middle finger touches the pen on the top or side (shown in the table as an increase in contact below or off). The difference between the 7 with 9 year olds and the 15 year olds is again statistically significant, ($X^2(1) = 5.0$, p<.05). No statistically significant effects of sex or preferred hand on the proportion using the modal feature were observed.

So far we have considered each penhold feature in isolation. However, any one person's penhold is defined by a combination of features. Thus, for example, Elliott and Connolly's 'dynamic tripod' penhold may be described as one in which the thumb and index finger act on opposite sides of the barrel, with the remaining digits below or off. This was observed in only about one third of the children in each age group (see Table 5).

Table 5 Percentage of children exhibiting 2 types of penhold.

Penhold	Age group		
	7	9	15
Dynamic tripod	34	37	38
Modified tripod	71	72	85

Ziviani (1983) suggests that this definition of tripod penhold may be broadened by the addition of those penholds with the middle finger on the barrel, and by relaxing the restriction on the positions of thumb and index finger. This means including penholds where the finger or thumb is on top of the pen rather than on the side. Some three-quarters of the children in our study had penholds satisfying this description of 'modified tripod' penhold. It is interesting to observe the proportion increases with age, the difference between the 7 with 9 year olds and the 15 year olds being statistically significant, $(X^2(1) = 5.98, p<.05)$.

Penhold and writing speed
The average writing speed for the first two sentences (written normally) taken together and the third sentence (written as fast as possible) are presented in Table 6 in terms of the number of characters written per minute. From 7 years to 9 years there is an increase in speed of approximately 50%, and from 9 years to 15 years of another 70%. All three age groups were able to speed up by about 25% when asked to write as fast as possible.

Table 6 Writing speed (in characters per minute) as a function of age.

Sentence	Age group		
	7	9	15
Average of (1) and (2)	46	64	117
(3)	55	82	140

The effects of the various penhold features on writing speed were assessed by comparing the writing of those children adopting the modal value of each penhold feature with the writing speed of the other children. In most cases no significant difference was found. The principal exception relates to the relative position of the thumb and index finger on the pen barrel. For 15 year old children, those with the index finger leading (nearer the writing point) wrote significantly faster, both when writing at a normal speed and when writing as fast as possible; for the latter measure, the average was 150 letters per minute against 136 letters per minute $(t(101) = 2.28, p<.05)$.

We found no significant advantage in terms of speed to writing with either the dynamic or modified tripods described in the preceding section. If anything, there was a slight trend in the opposite direction.

Discussion

This study shows that it is possible to describe penholds in a systematic and detailed fashion suitable for quantitative analysis. Our data show two main differences between the penholds actually used by schoolchildren in Britain today and those commonly illustrated in writing manuals. One was that in over 60% of children the distal interphalangeal joint of the index finger was hyperextended. This suggests perhaps that the majority of children hold their pens too tightly. The other was the surprising number of children (65%) who write with their thumbs closest to the pen tip (writing manuals usually suggest that the index finger should lead). Although not formally quantified, we have also observed that the digit nearest to the tip of the pen was usually considerably closer than would normally be recommended by teachers. One consequence of this might be a reduction in visual feedback from the pen trace as it is produced.

The speed values that we report are somewhat faster than those presented by Groff (1961). This probably reflects the different letterform models in use in the two countries and the shorter texts used in the present study. In our study we looked at the ability to write faster on demand, finding similar percentage increases at different ages. This represents a surprisingly large reserve capacity and points to the need for the researcher to give explicit instruction when trying to assess handwriting proficiency in terms of speed.

Despite the large changes in writing speed with age over individuals we only found two points of evolution of grip with age: index finger less often on the side and middle finger less often on top/touching side.

To us, a surprising finding was that there appears to be little cost to adopting an unconventional, *i.e.* non-modal, penhold feature at least in terms of speed of writing. However, of course writing speed should not be the only criterion: legibility is clearly likely to be at issue. Thus work is at present in hand to examine the effects of non-modal penholds on letter formation.

One implication of the relative lack of effect of penhold, at least on writing speed, is that a child writing with an unconventional penhold would not necessarily do better to adopt a more conventional grip. In this context it is interesting to note Otto, *et al* (1966) study showing that adults are able to adopt a modified grip with the pen lying between the index and middle fingers with little difficulty. In our study only one child, a 9 year old girl, had spontaneously adopted this penhold. After assessment this penhold was tried out with those secondary school pupils who complained of pain while writing. On the whole they found that it helped considerably. This way of holding a pen can also prove helpful in certain neurological conditions, for example, where it may be unsatisfactory for someone to adopt a dynamic tripod.

One aspect of penhold that we have not classified up to now but which we feel deserves examination is where on the hand is the highest point of contact with the pen. While many modern instruction manuals would advocate the web between the index finger and thumb we have often observed it lying closer toward the proximal interphalangeal joint of the index finger which causes the pen to be held more upright. In the present study we have only described the way the pen is held and have not attempted to document the dynamics of the writing movements.

The full text of this paper appears in French in the book of the proceedings of that conference; (Sassoon, in Sirat, Poule and Irigoin 1990)

IMPLICATIONS AND APPLICATIONS OF AN ANALYSIS OF PENHOLD

A study of this depth understandably leads to further thought. An opportunity arose for another presentation on the same subject at a conference in May 1988, at the CNRS. (Centre Nationale de la Recherche Scientifique) Paris. The following excerpts from that presentation expand on the issues involved in penhold.

The effect of the writing implement and the penhold on the written trace should be taken into consideration in any serious investigation into handwriting. The analysis of penholds reported in Sassoon, Wing and Nimmo-Smith (1986) broke new ground. The classification set out to determine some of the essential factors that would permit description and quantification not only of unconventional penholds but the details of what might loosely be termed conventional penholds as well. This type of classification can be extended to include any additional factors that might be necessary for a future study. For example, it became evident when testing the older age groups that, for some purposes the size of the hand, in particular the measurement from web to the thumb or index finger-tip, might be relevant. Therefore tracings of each writer's hand was taken. (They remain to be analysed.)

Observations indicated that that certain aspects of penhold altered as the hand travelled along the line. Any further analysis might be designed to take this into account. A video would throw up other factors for investigation such as consistency of penhold throughout a page of writing. The position of the paper in relation to the midline of the body, and the angle of the paper in relation to the edge of the desk are other factors likely to influence penhold. These positions were noted and quantified in our survey.

It was evident from the data that in terms of writing time that unconventional penholds fared slightly better than conventional ones. Simple observation (and personal experimentation) however, show that certain penholds inhibit the writer's freedom to form certain strokes, thus influencing the written trace. These are the first points to discuss:

1 If unconventional penholds worked just as well as the conventional tripod grip, and in some cases better, then the reason must be found. The pupils in this survey all used a ballpoint pen for their written task. When the photographs of some of the most extreme penholds were examined one solution was immediately suggested. The elevation of the ballpoint pen was more upright than is ever recommended for the use of a pencil or traditional fountain pen. Many modern pens only function when held a relatively upright angle. Moreover as the pens near the end of their useful lives they require an even more upright position in order to produce any trace on the paper. Whether or not children are permitted to use felt-tipped or ballpoint pens during their early years at school, most children learn their mark-making strategies at home, and continue to draw and write outside school hours using modern pens. I would not wish to give the impression that these pens should not be used, but that we should consider whether the penholds that were recommended for pencils and traditional

fountain pens are suitable for modern pens. There are many historical precedents for the prescription for penhold being changed when a new form of writing implement was introduced. I would suggest that we have ignored the lessons of history by introducing pens that have different points and therefore require different prescription for usage, without sufficient (if any) research. Until such work is undertaken I believe that children will themselves be trying to formulate their own strategies. In addition they may meet with opposition from their teachers as they attempt to adjust the position and pressures of their fingers within a conventional framework, to use a pen that needs to be held almost upright. One possible alternative strategy has been well researched, although it was for a different purpose, by the Belgian neurologist Callewaert. The penhold that he suggested for the release of tension also allows a pen to write at almost any elevation without strain on the fingers. Some adults and children too, adopt this position spontaneously. Maybe it is time for educationists to consider this more seriously.

An alternative penhold *left;* one nine-year-old in my survey used this alternative penhold. Illustration from Sassoon (1986). *right;* A similar penhold illustrated in Callewaert (1962).

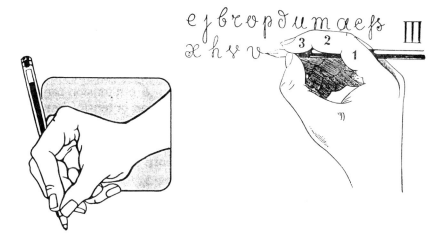

2 We need to research the effects of penhold on the written trace. This analysis was only the first step. It had been hoped that the analysis of penhold could be combined with the analysis of written strokes of the same subjects, and that some conclusions might be reached. However the variability of penholds revealed, even in our sample of three hundred, was such that it became

evident that a much larger and more specific sample was needed. This would mean a set number of people who were accustomed to using each of a variety of penholds.

Many handwriting studies can be, and are, undertaken in laboratory conditions. It has been suggested that such a study could be conducted with subjects trying to imitate the various penholds and testing their efficiency and/or their effect on the written trace. I feel that this not only simplifies a complex situation but could not produce valid conclusions. We can only guess at the causes of some unconventional penholds, and note that those who use them may find them to work well, whereas those who imitate them find them awkward. Modern pens have been cited as one possible factor (in the development of unconventional penholds). Hand size and personal tensions are among other factors to consider as well as the changes necessitated by having to write at speed, while content, spelling and grammar etc. only add to the pressures that transmit themselves via the hand to the page.

The implications of this first study should be important for educationists and document examiners, and the applications are of use in particular in medical diagnoses. Pain when writing is becoming a real problem for children and adults alike. The survey that led up to this analysis of penholds revealed that 40% of the fifteen year old girls, and 25% of the boys suffered pain when writing. Another project, looking into the causes of writer's cramp, (reported in Chapters 6 and 7), revealed that a high proportion of those people suffered pain before they became unable to write. The classification would allow a data base of penholds of writer's cramp patients to be built up.

Research is needed in the field just as much as in the laboratory. We need to know what is happening to our children in the classroom and to adults who need to write later in life. The findings to date suggest that the unconventional penholds may be individual's strategies for coming to terms with modern pens. Whatever prescription is made for teaching penhold, individuals will probably adapt it to their own needs. If we adher only to traditional concepts, whether in penhold, letterform or the task of writing itself today, we will be letting down yet another generation of students.

This section discusses the ongoing effects of this analysis of penhold on my own work and on my perception of penhold both in educational and more therapeutic situations.

MORE ABOUT PENHOLD

Several years later there is a little more to say. Penhold provides a complicated series of factors that, in real life, have to be observed and analysed simultaneously. These different actions, pressures and postures can be difficult to interpret without a framework to separate important elements of the penhold, both when static and in motion. The analysis was developed by studying photographs of the three hundred pupils involved in my survey. Having established some of the different elements that influenced how the pen was operated, it became progressively easier to separate and diagnose which elements of penhold might be inhibiting writing or causing individuals to experience pain. Although that might not have been the initial purpose of the analysis of penhold, it had been for me, one of its most practical consequences. It has taught me to see how the many elements of fingers, hand and arm inter-relate, and how to explain clearly and concisely to patients the way that their actions may be disadvantageous to them. It can then be suggested in what direction they might experiment themselves to find a more appropriate writing strategy. In no way has this work led me to suppose that there is an ideal penhold to recommend. To the contrary. It seems to have highlighted that different body proportions and personal pressures, when allied to the many differences in size, shape and points of modern writing implements provide such a multiplicity of factors that it is better to suggest a variety of penholds for experimentation. This means a much more open and informed attitude to penhold is needed than is now universally to be found.

There are several ongoing effects of this paper.

1 The analysis apart, the statistical findings that unconventional penholds could be faster than conventional ones, proved a turning point in my own attitude to prescribing penhold. I no longer had any reservation in suggesting unconventional penholds as alternatives. I was exposed to even more extreme penholds adopted by those with severe hand deformity, who had found excellent strategies for themselves. These seemed to work well, whichever web, even that between the fourth and little finger, was employed. With more confidence it was possible to help those with minimal function to write quite happily, two-handedly.

These patients successes have taught me to have even less respect for conventional rules of penhold, and I can only hope that my writings in the intervening years has helped others to widen their observations.

2 It was considered necessary to put into the paper that we had not tabulated any differences in the quality of handwriting produced by unconventional penholds. I still believe as I did then that it is not only impossible to try to assess 'quality' but also undesirable. The aspects that are judged to represent quality are so personal and coloured so much by the judges's perception and expectation, as to be not only useless, but often misleading. In educational terms, this can also be dangerous. If quality, like legibility, is likely to be in the mind of the perceiver, then such judgements are hardly likely to encourage the experimentation, either with pens or letterforms, that is so essential is we are to find a handwriting for the future needs of our students. A quality judgement is likely to be a conventional one.

Extreme penholds may distort or inhibit the written trace. The same inhibitions can be found in the trace of pupils who use a conventional penhold too stiffly. Given a set of previously written examples, however, it would be difficult to detect whether any particular writer had a conventional or unconventional penhold. This can only be confirmed when the writer is seen in action. Undoubtedly radical alterations in penhold involve alterations in the resulting trace. More relaxed penholds, whether relatively conventional or completely unconventional, produce more relaxed writing. If the ability to speed up the writing now the hand can function more freely, produces a less neat writing, because the writer manages at last to keep up with note-taking or writes more in the same time – is it logical then to describe this as less good quality? I am involved in assessing needs in the real world and have no wish to be involved with tabulating qualities that do not take into account the realities of the act of writing and the needs of the writer as dictated by usage.

3 The speed has other implications. The limitations of formal papers, indeed such a wide-ranging project itself, precluded investigation into how penhold altered as the sample relaxed into faster more unconscious scribble. The difference in slant and proportion of the letterforms is discussed elsewhere. Alteration of

penhold in different circumstance and over a period of time deserve more attention.

4 The pain survey that was used with one hundred fifteen year old pupils provided a possible link between hand size and pain. This is commented on in the paper on writer's cramp and also deserves more research. It requires anatomical measurements that I am not equipped or informed enough to take. Moreover I have discussed this matter with several experts in the field of hand development and no-one has been able to decide which measurements would be most appropriate to take to provide valid evidence on this aspect of penhold. I sincerely hope that someone will take up this challenge one day.

There are other more subtle points that deserve a mention here – again for discussion and not provable in the way required by academic papers. I gained a gradual realisation of how penhold, indeed any aspect of writing posture is an indication of the writer's whole makeup. It is therefore a useful diagnostic aid. An unconventional penhold may be symbolic, conversely a conventional person may, initially reject an unconventional penhold even though, rationally he may see it to be beneficial. In such cases historical references and illustrations may help. I have

The alternative penhold suited this writer who had rather long fingers.

also come to realise that the recommended change to an alternative penhold need not be permanent. Once it has done its job, perhaps helping a stressed student through examinations, it may no longer be necessary. Individuals who have followed this route have demonstrated this. Once they have relaxed, their conventional penhold which was tortuous and painful under stress, works well again for them, and they may prefer to revert to it.

I have found anecdotal evidence most useful over a period of time. Teachers and therapists would do well to embark on some gentle questioning before condemning extreme penholds. – 'I started writing like this when I broke my index finger, how odd that I still do it' – a girl who used a tripod grip involving thumb, middle finger and ring finger.

'I use two fingers because I find it easier to control the pen' – a girl whose hand was supinated (on edge) in such a way that it would be difficult to write with the pen supported by only one finger. I could go on for several pages with such comments.

It is difficult for me to estimate whether this time-consuming analysis has proven useful to other researchers. I feel that any further work that is undertaken in this field is likely to be more anatomical, thus further away from the natural and personal act of writing. But for me and my own purposes and growth, the value of all this work has been inestimable, and I am grateful to my colleagues at the MRC APU who made it all possible.

CHAPTER 3

Variability of Letters

Introduction

Handwriting is a combination of the visible trace of a hand movement while the pen is on the paper and the invisible trace of the movements when the pen is not in contact with the paper. Together this is called the ductus of writing, a paleographic term. There is much to be learned from paleographic studies of the changing ductus of certain letters in our alphabet. Many so-called personal variations of contemporary letters are variations that are consequences of minor changes in ductus that have been taught and generally used in other centuries or are even now in use in other countries.

Our education system, along with most others, does not appreciate the desirability and inevitability of personal variations in handwriting. Standard letters, which often follow whatever model is in fashion, are taught and praised. While it is imperative that the correct movement of basic letters should be carefully taught and corrected from the start, the small alterations in ductus that lead to what might be termed shortcuts within or between letters (once they are joined), are seldom recognised. If recognised they would be more likely to be criticised than praised. These slight differences often arise as a consequence of variation in proportion and slant of letters, which in themselves are influenced by the way individual writers use their bodies, and their individual pressures. In other cases, such as with complex letters such as 't', 'f' and 'k', there may be other forces at work.

There is a considerable body of work, mostly from the field of forensic document examining, that looks at certain variations of letters within and between writers. Inevitably, I was interested in the work that had just taken place in the MRC APU by Eldridge, Nimmo-Smith, Wing and Totty (1984), although my focus was different. It was developmental and educational rather than from a forensic angle. The crossbar join provides a useful field for study with the variations of the 'th' crossbar easier to analyse that the very complex variations that arise from the letter f.

The word 'the' was included in both the fast and slow test sentences in my research survey. Several other crossbar combinations that would be interesting for comparison were also included. Even a casual glance through the examples that were collected showed a wide variation in the ductus of 'th' as written in the word 'the'. There were some particularly interesting ones produced by left-handers, and even children as young as seven had found ingenious solutions to a crossbar join.

There were exciting differences between examples of fast and slow writing within individuals, but it took quite a complex analysis to evaluate the extent of the variations.

DEVELOPING EFFICIENCY IN CURSIVE HANDWRITING

An analysis of 't' crossing behaviour in children

Speed with legibility is often taken to be the goal of handwriting. The emphasis on speed is particularly strongly felt in the secondary school as children of 15 and 16 are assessed on their academic ability through a series of written examinations. In these, the children often have to work under considerable time pressure and it is probably the case that slower writers are at some disadvantage. Certainly teachers in secondary school often have to point out to their pupils the need for fast as well as legible handwriting.

Various motoric factors may contribute to improving the speed of handwriting. In Sassoon, Nimmo-Smith and Wing (1986) we have considered the possible contribution of penhold to the speed of handwriting. In the present paper we consider how improved efficiency in handwriting might also result from changes in the manner in which one letter is joined or connected to another letter.

In English schools the taught form of the letter 't' consists of two separate strokes. First a vertical downstroke is used to produce an upright that then leads into a base formed by an anticlockwise curve. Following a pen lift, the crossbar is then added as a horizontal line drawn across the upright (i.e. $\mathcal{t}$). Normally, this form of construction will be employed because when teaching

This paper was presented at the Third Conference of the International Graphonomics Society in Montreal. It was first published as Sassoon R, Nimmo-Smith I and Wing AM (1989) in *Computer Recognition and Human Production of Handwriting*, eds. Plamondon R, Suen CY and Simner M pp. 287-97. It is reproduced here by kind permission of my co-authors and World Scientific Publishing Co. Singapore.

children cursive writing, the curved base of the 't' is simply extended to the next letter without the need to lift the pen (i.e. *th*).
From an instructional perspective this is considered appropriate in
that the connecting stroke to the next letter originates near the
writing line in a manner similar to that taught for most of the other
letters of the alphabet. However, if this curved base join is
employed, there arises the problem of the crossbar which is needed
to complete the 't'. Specifically, the writer must later return,
perhaps from the end of the word, to the upright for the 't' and
add the required crossbar.

There are problems associated with a crossbar formed in this
manner. The movement required to bring the pen back to a
position near the top of the upright takes time in proportion to the
distance between the upright and the end of the word. The longer
the word, the greater will be the loss of writing speed. The time
lost in this way will be particularly severe if the writer attempts to
place the left end of the crossbar accurately against the upright.
One way the writer can resolve the difficultly created by the 't'
crossbar formed in this manner is to construct the crossbar prior to
connecting the 't' to the next letter in a word. But if, after forming
the crossbar, the writer returns to the curved base of the 't' and
repositions the pen so as to avoid a break in the line, this
repositioning will itself incur a time penalty.

For these reasons it would seem advantageous for the writer to
substitute the crossbar in place of the curved base as the point of
origin in connecting the 't' to the following letter (i.e. *the*). Such a
change in letter construction should lend itself to faster
handwriting because the writer does not need to return to the 't'
after completing the word. Indeed, the use of the crossbar to join
't' with the following 'h' may be seen in many English adult
writers even though it was not taught in this way in schools (see
Figure 1).

In an analysis of the variability of selected categorical features in
adult cursive handwriting, Eldridge *et al* (1983) included data on
'th' joins. They reported joins by base in 55% of cases and by
crossbar in 27%. Interestingly, they noted that in the word 'the' the
crossbar join is potentially one of the most powerful features
available to the forensic document examiner. This conclusion was
based on an index that expresses variability within any one

individual's handwriting relative to variability observed between individuals. This index could be said to embody the concept of 'personal style' in handwriting. The crossbar join is a 'good' forensic feature because people allow themselves individuality in the form of join they use despite having been originally taught the same form.

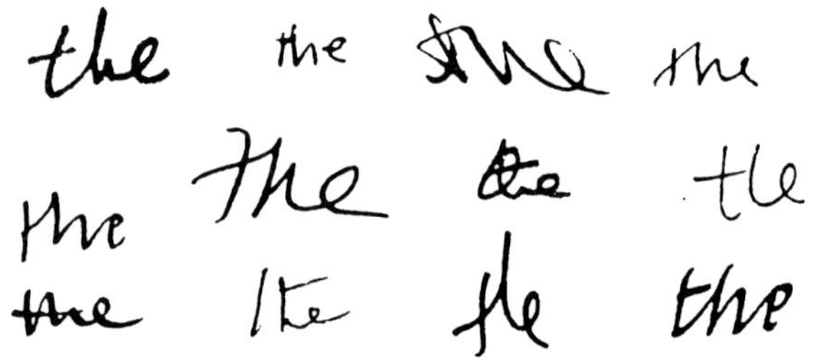

Figure 1
Examples of the word 'the' written by adults showing personal variations of crossbar and baseline joining. Reproduced from Sassoon and Briem (1984).

In this paper we report evidence showing clearly that children do increasingly favour the crossbar join over the taught join from the base as they become proficient writers. Furthermore, when children are asked to write quickly, many of those who do not otherwise use this alternative pattern tend to do so. We believe the outcome of the present investigation questions the usefulness of approaches to the teaching of handwriting that fail to take account of the natural evolution of letter form as skill progresses. Instead, we suggest that taught letter forms should lend themselves more easily to modifications that many children will themselves eventually discover as they seek more efficient styles of writing.

Method

Samples of handwriting were obtained from 394 English schoolchildren (14% left-handed) distributed among four age groups (7–8, 9–10, 12–13 and 15–16 years). The two younger age groups came from six primary schools, five of them in the catchment area for the two secondary schools that provided the two older groups. The seven, nine and fifteen-year-old age groups comprised the children whose pen grips were reported in Sassoon, Nimmo-Smith and Wing (1986).

The children were tested individually and asked to carry out a simple written task. The primary school children were read three sentences averaging eight words apiece. The first two sentences, repeated three times each, were given to each child on a typed card and written at normal speed. The last sentence was a line from a familiar nursery rhyme and the children were asked to write this once, as fast as possible. A word 'the', which appeared in the first and third sentence, provided three examples of the 'th' connection when written at normal speed and one example at enhanced speed. For the two remaining groups of secondary school pupils the three test sentences contained on average ten words. Here the word 'the' appeared in the second and third sentences. The first two sentences were repeated twice only, as less rehearsal was considered necessary for the secondary pupils. Thus children in the two older groups provided two examples of 'the' written at normal speed, and one example at enhanced speed.

Three of the primary schools used the formal published handwriting models of Fagg, Worthy and Richardson. The other primary schools developed their own handwriting models which were very similar to these. In all six schools, the letter 't' was taught with a vertical downstroke leading into a base formed by an anticlockwise curve and a join between 't' and 'h' that consisted of a line starting from the base of the 't'. Figure 2 shows the word 'the' as represented in the three models.

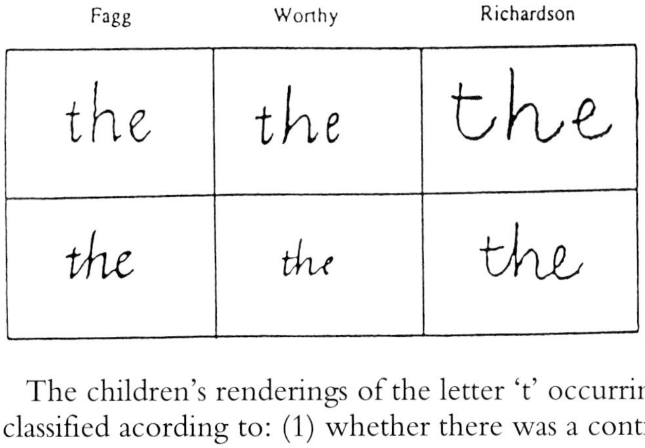

Figure 2
Models, shown in Fagg, Worthy and Richardson, for forming the word 'the' are first illustrated in separate letters and then in cursive to show the recommended baseline join.

Fagg	Worthy	Richardson
the	the	the
the	the	the

The children's renderings of the letter 't' occurring in 'the' were classified acording to: (1) whether there was a continuous written trace between some part of the 't' and the 'h', or whether a break in the trace was evident; (2) if the trace was continuous, whether the join to the following letter stemmed from the base of the 't' or from the crossbar; and (3) whether the bottom of the upright of the 't' curved into an anticlockwise base or whether the upright was straight at the bottom (possibly with a retrace).

Results

Figure 3 provides examples of normal and fast handwriting for each age group. Variation in the joining stroke between 't' and 'h' is apparent both as a function of age and speed of writing. We first turn to a statistical analysis of the effects of age on the normal speed of handwriting.

Table 1 shows the percentage of children in each age group who exhibited a continuous trace between 't' and 'h'. A large increase from age seven to nine contrasts with a slight dip from age nine to ten and recovery from age twelve to fifteen, $(x^2(3) = 42.70$, $p<0.01)$. Individual pairwise chi-square tests showed that the significance of the overall chi-square was due to the relatively few seven-year-olds using continuous joins. The effect is even more pronounced when data from seven- and nine-year-olds at one

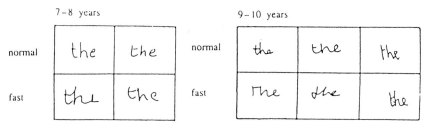

Figure 3
Examples of the word 'the' written at normal and fast speeds by children at the ages of 7, 9,12, and 15.

primary school, teaching the Marion Richardson method which encourages continuous cursive from the age of five, were omitted (see figures in parentheses).

Table 2 shows the percentage of children employing a curved base, as a function of age. A monotonic decline is seen with age, with a particularly large drop between ages nine and twelve, $(x^2(3) = 50.15, p<0.01)$. Individual pairwise chi-square tests revealed that the differences were significant between ages seven and nine and between ages nine and twelve, but not between ages twelve and fifteen.

Table 3 gives the percentage of children who used a continuous join and employed: (1) a straight 't', which implies a crossbar join; $(x^2(3) = 18.76, p<0.01)$, (2) a curved base 't' *and* a crossbar join $(x^2(3) = 21.03, p<0.01)$.

Pairwise chi-square tests for percentage straight 't' showed the increases with age were significant except from age seven to nine. For percentage curved and joined by crossbar the only significant pair-wise increase with age was between nine and twelve.

The effect of asking the children to write as fast as possible is summarised in Table 4. This table contrasts the number of children who changed to a crossbar join having not employed a crossbar join at normal speed ('gains') with the number of children who ceased using a crossbar join at speed ('losses'). In each group, except the nine-year-olds, gains exceed losses at or beyond the .05 level of significance by McNemar's test for matched pairs of binary responses.

Table 1 Joins between th' as a function of age (the figures in parentheses are obtained by omitting from the analysis, the primary school employing the Marion Richardson method)

| | Age group (years) | | | |
	7	9	12	15
Number in group	92 (72)	99 (79)	103	103
Percentage continuous join	18.5 (1.3)	59.8 (53.3)	49.0	59.2

Table 2 Employment of curved base in 't' as a function of age

| | Age group (years) | | | |
	7	9	12	15
Percentage curved base	97.8 (97.3)	89.9 (87.3)	70.0	63.1

Table 3 Type of join as a function of age given continuous join between 't' and 'h'

| | Age group (years) | | | |
	7	9	12	15
Percentage straight	0 (0)	5.2 (7.1)	16.3	31.1
Percentage curved and join by crossbar	0 (0)	3.6 (5.1)	24.4	31.0

Table 4 The effect of writing as fast as possible on use of the crossbar join. Gains refer to the number of children employing a crossbar join between 'th' when they did not do so at normal speed, losses to the number who used a crossbar join at normal speed but did not do so when writing as fast as possible.

| | Age group (years) | | | |
	7	9	12	15
Gains	5 (3)	4 (3)	20	12
Losses	0 (0)	1 (1)	3	4

Discussion

This study shows there are systematic changes with age in the use of the continuous trace join between 't' and the following 'h'. The changes may be summarised in the following way. *From seven to nine years,* the children largely follow the instructional model as they learn to join without pen lift so that there is little decline in use of the curved base. Of those employing a continuous join at age nine, relatively few do so using the crossbar. *From nine to twelve years*, the children acquire some freedom in writing style and there is a decline in use of the curved base. This decline is associated with a drop in use of the continuous join by the base that is not compensated for by the rise in the use of the crossbar join implied by the straight 't'. However, amongst those using a curved base and employing a continuous join there is a notable increase in crossbar joining. *From twelve to fifteen years,* there is a further decline in the use of the curved base as a form of joining. The use of the crossbar join increases.

In the introduction it was pointed out that as children get older they are under increasing pressure to write faster. It would, therefore, seem plausible to suppose that the observed changes in 'th' joining are related to the need to develop an efficient joining movement in writing; one which would facilitate greater speed without serious loss in legibility. The interpretation that the changes in joining are related to speed receives support from the fact that when children were instructed to write as fast as possible, there was a direct increase in use of crossbar joining. A change in the form of 'th' join taught at school would thus certainly seem warranted.

Figure 4
An example of the Italian hand written by Martin Billingsley from *The Pen's Excellence* (1618). Below an enlargement of the word 'the' showing the crossbar join.

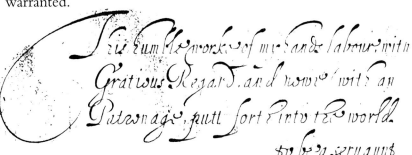

Writing masters in past centuries taught several variations of the crossbar join to both the letters 'f' and 't'. Some could be considered to be more for embellishment than efficiency. The writing master Martin Billingsley taught King Charles I in his

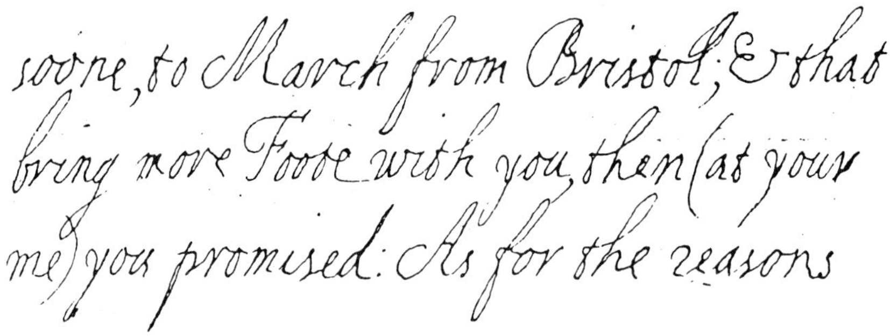

soone, to March from Bristol; & that
bring more Foote with you, then (as your
me) you promised: As for the reasons

Figure 5
An example of the
handwriting of King
Charles 1 who had been
a student of Billingsley.
Written in 1644, this
shows consistent
crossbar joins from 't'.
An enlargement of the
word 'the' shows his
crossbar join.

youth. Illustrations of the Italian hand from Billingsley's *The Pen's Excellence* of 1618 (Figure 4) contrast with the king's mature hand written in 1644 (Figure 5). The latter shows a consistent personalised variation of the crossbar join from the letter 't' quite different from Billingsley's model.

An illustration of a round hand alphabet dating from approximately 1670 is shown in Figure 6. It clearly illustrates a retrace crossbar from a straight 't'.

abcddefgghiklmnopqrstuvwxyz

Figure 7 shows handwriting samples written with quill pen from a series of writing books of the late eighteenth and early nineteenth centuries in the possession of the first author. These samples, written by a curate BG, show variations of crossbar joins from the letter 't'. In the case of his writing as a young child, it may be assumed that the joins were copied from a master or a copy book. Over a period of years, a progression in BG's writing may be seen in the development of 'th' ligatures.

For more recent approaches to the joining of 't' with the following letter, we turn to two current instructional books (see Figure 8). Barnard suggested a horizontal crossbar join as a link to the following tall letter but in fact used a baseline join for 'th' throughout his copy books. Jarman stressed that the cross strokes of both 'f' and 't' should be made 'at the height of the minims 'u', 'm', 'n', etc. as they will eventually become fast economical joins'. Horizontal joins to these 'minims' appeared in his copy books but he consistently used a baseline join for 'th'.

Despite the continued emphasis on teaching baseline joins, our

Figure 6
A roundhand alphabet
dating from 1670
illustrating a crossbar
join from 't' and an
enlargement of the join
between 'tu'. (The
illustrations on this page
are reproduced from
Whalley 1969.)

Figure 7
The development of the handwriting of a curate, BG, between 1799 and 1820, from a child's copybook, through school exercise books to a mature hand employed in writing a diary.
Inset: Enlargements of the word 'the' in the four stages of writing to show the development of crossbar joins. (From original material in the possession of RS.)

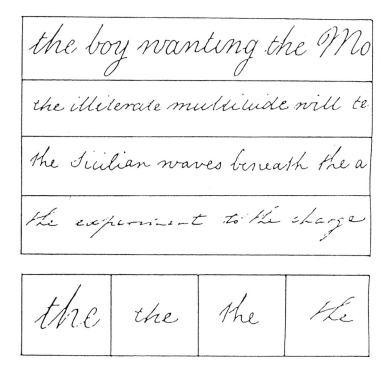

data show that at the age of 15, of the 59% of children joining 't' and 'h'] (Table 1), 62% join by crossbar (Table 3). It is interesting to contrast these data with the observations of Eldridge *et al* (1983). The adults in their study, whose ages ranged from 22 to 68, joined 't' and 'h' in 82% of cases; of these only 33% were joins by crossbar. It appears that the individual's search for efficient forms of joining stroke in handwriting is improved, perhaps due to greater freedom to experiment, in today's schoolchildren.

Figure 8
Examples from instructional materials by Jarman and Barnard. Both writers give exercises to teach a join from the crossbar in some circumstances, but consistently demonstrate a baseline join in the word 'the'.

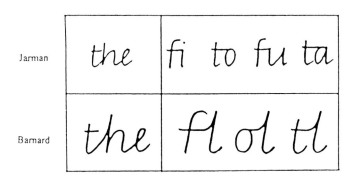

The discussion would not be complete without some consideration of the left-handed writer. As documented, for example, by Franks *et al* (1985), left-handers show significant differences from right-handers in the stroke direction of certain letters. In particular, for a large sample of adult writers (i.e. age 15 and upwards) they found nearly 60% of the left-handers using a right-to-left crossbar. Over the age groups in the present study, the percentage of left-handers using a right-to-left crossbar was 82%. Although the number of left-handers in the present study was too small to allow a formal analysis, examination of the individual cases did indicate that left-handers had some extra difficulty in achieving efficiency in using the crossbar join.

In conclusion we suggest that departures from the taught model for 't' in handwriting reflect a general search for efficient letterforms by the writer. The possibility of such an optimisation process, which may not necessarily operate at a conscious level, warrants further research. This would be preferably of a longitudinal nature so that the way particular children shift between different letterforms over an extended period may be evaluated. We believe that questions about how and why departures from the taught form arise will prompt educationalists to reconsider the taught models used in handwriting instruction.

THE IMPLICATIONS OF PERSONAL LETTERFORMS

The implications are discussed further and other letters looked at in several different ways. A new analysis of the letter 'k' suggests a method of tabulating variability. Exercises are shown which can be used to demonstrate to writers the variability of their own hand.

It is worth examining some of the ideas and practical experiments that have arisen from this work, and to look at how easily it might be extended. Today this is not only of interest to education and forensic studies but to the rapidly expanding study of computer recognition of letters. In this field the Japanese and US researchers seem to find many less variations of letters or joins because of more formal continuous cursive national handwriting models and stricter teaching methods. This work, undertaken in England at a time of much more lax attitudes to handwriting models, indicates more clearly the individuality and efficiency that may occur to the benefit of the individual writer as a result of experimentation with letters. In some circles this might be viewed as disadvantageous to the regularity and recognition factors of a more formalised hand.

Several other matters have been brought up by these analyses, some of which have been of practical use in explaining to others my own theories of the benefits of personal deviations.

1 That permitted to experiment (or not too closely supervised) many children find variations of letters and joins on their own and use them appropriately in particular positions in words, as described by Wing, Nimmo-Smith and Eldridge (1983).

2 That most people (adults and children alike) are unaware of the variations in their letterforms, and when asked to reproduce them specifically are often awkward in their writing of such a letter, or unable to repeat what they have happily used, perhaps in several instances, in unconscious writing. Another related point is to consider what variations within or between letters may tell one about the individual writer. Without making too many generalisations, it may separate those who are able or willing for whatever reason to explore unconventional strategies for the sake of either efficiency or even individuality, from those who are unable or unwilling to do so. I use the 'th' crossbar join as an indicator when examining a handwriting. It suggests to me an enquiring and less conventional personality, and, however poor a child's writing, it is the first thing that I notice and praise. It is essential not to base too much on such judgements, and it is important to remember that the strict teaching of continuous cursive would minimise opportunity for children to experiment. In addition, those who have to teach a standard hand may have had to train themselves carefully to eliminate such personal variations.

3 The paper indicated that such crossbar variations appear more frequently when writing at speed, and where such crossbars may have been used in normal writing the efficiency of these joins was sometimes increased at speed. The implications for the motor programming of such variations of movement within and between letters at speed surely deserves further investigation. The implications for education are reasonably clear. Without experimentation there would be no repertoire of choice between

the more formal but less efficient forms, and those most efficient therefore more suitable at speed. An investigation into the storage and retrieval of such alternatives requires a finer and more scientific study than I am able to carry out, but it remains a fascinating possibility.

4 The analysis of these examples has left one problem unresolved. At what stage does a personal variation of a letter so degrade the identity of the letter that it becomes unrecognisable? In the case of the crossbar from 't' to 'h' this occurred occasionally when the so-called crossbar started at, or near, the baseline, and was detached from the stem of the letter 't'. Had such instances been viewed out of context it would not have been easy to identify them as the letter 't'. (That is assuming that everyone would agree that the characteristics of a letter 't' are that it consists of an upright or stem stroke and a crossbar. These characteristics differentiate a letter 't' from a slightly lengthened letter 'i' or a slightly shortened letter 'l'.)
    Before leaving the subject of the variation of letters within this specific sample, I would like to include a few ideas from an unfinished and therefore obviously unpublished paper on the variation of the letter 'k'. Several separate instances of the letter, both at normal speed and at fast speed, had been included in the test sentences. In addition the word 'kicked' had been included in the sentences for the younger children, and the words 'keys' and 'monkeys' in the older sample. This enabled me to look for instances of different usage within a word as well as between words or at speed. I began an analysis of the variation in usage of forms of the letter 'k', then the visual analysis of those different form. This was great fun. A schematic table of the numerous variations is shown here, but the problem of when a particular letter loses its identity through shortcuts still remained. Ian Nimmo-Smith and I started thinking about an idea for a grid to help in the description of the elements and proportions that are essential for the recognition of separate letters. I am purposely not using the word 'legibility' here. This is because the actual legibility of written letters may be less specific. It can depend on context as well as the suggestion of features of letters, rather than the actual presence of such features. We never found time to pursue this idea further than to relate it to the letter 'k'.

Variations of the letter 'k'.

Line 1 written in one stroke

Lines 2 and 3 written with two strokes - the last two are sequenced in such a way as to preclude their joining to a following letter.

Line 4 written with three separate strokes

Lines 5 and 6 would not be considered acceptable according to the grid system of recognition explained on page 55.

All these variations were found within the handwriting of approximately four hundred school children between the ages of seven and sixteen. All the children attended one of six primary schools or two secondary schools in the same district.

Where judgements are being made about the increasing efficiency of personal variations of letterforms, there remains a problem concerning a cut-off point when the identity of any letter may be so eroded as to cease to be a fair representation of that letter. This very point arose in Sassoon, Wing and Nimmo-Smith (1987) where crossbar joins in the word 'the' were being classified. A visual judgement had to be made in a few cases when the change of direction of the initial stroke came so close to the baseline as to cease to be a crossbar join, being classifiable only as a baseline join. In other words the letter, if viewed in isolation, would no longer be identifiable as a 't' as it appeared to have no crossbar.

It is not the intention to define the most desirable form of the letter 'k' to be taught in schools. However, it is possible to give some indication of the features of the letter that are acceptable, both in static shape or in movement terms, that might affect the identity of the letter. The other letters within our alphabet that are most likely to be confused with the letter 'k' must first be identified. It can then be shown what elements must be present or absent in order to differentiate between them and the letter 'k'.

1 The height differentials must be maintained in order to differentiate between a capital 'K' and a small 'k', or a capital 'R' in the case of a closed 'k'.

2 A change of direction must be indicated in the lower right-hand segment of the letter 'k' to differentiate between it and the letter 'h', but this change of direction should not be so low as to cause confusion between the letters 'b' and 'k'.

3 This point concerns movement. The second part of the 'k' is best written in such a way as to terminate at the baseline in order to facilitate a baseline join. That would ensure that any ensuing ligature should be recognisable.

In the following visual analysis certain letters covered by points 1 and 2 will have to be classified as unacceptable as they do not conform to the necessary recognition criteria, although they may be more efficient in terms of strokes and legible within their context. Certain letters covered by point 3 may have to be classified as having an undesirable if not incorrect movement despite being recognisable and, as a letter in isolation, not necessarily any less efficient.

Before it is possible to judge if a personal variation could be termed acceptable or not, it seems necessary to define the characteristics of each letter in such a way as to pinpoint those that are essential to its identity. Verbal descriptions are at best clumsy, and existing terminology is not always precise enough for this purpose. It also varies between different disciplines.

The letter 'k' is one of the most distinctive of the letters in our alphabet, so the verbal description of unacceptable variations already described might be sufficient to identify most deviations for the purpose of this paper. Because of its very distinctiveness, the letter 'k' provides a useful opportunity to experiment with a simple numerical descriptive system for handwritten letters that might lead to a clearer understanding of permissable variations. The way that 'k' is segmented, vertically and horizontally, suggests a rectangular grid system. This grid could be further subdivided to describe in greater detail any segment or segments of a particular letter that differentiates it from any other. How the essential parts of each letter could be described is another matter. Numerical values would avoid the complicated terminology that would otherwise be needed. We pondered over the features of the various forms of the letter 'k' that were revealed in the preliminary survey of this small sample. All the forms investigated produced three spaces in its relevant rectangle. This is but a start; it might be difficult to define the essentials of the many variables of the letter 's', but most others would be relatively straightforward to define by this system.

This visual analysis illustrates the wide variety of forms of the letter 'k' found in this particular sample of three hundred children. There was an astonishing variety of forms within pupils from six schools where either one or other of the two common models was taught consistently – the open one similar to the capital form or the closed one written without a penlift. There were many examples of usage of different forms within the writing of individuals showing usage of different forms within different positions of the same word. In some instances there was evidence of increased efficiency at speed. There was also some evidence to suggest that the number of strokes (from one to three) used to produce this particular letter might be an indicator of graphic development within young children. However, at a later stage, 40% of the children who had been taught exclusively to use the

Personal shortcuts in adult handwriting.

I write like this when I want to make a good impression
I wrote like this when I'm in a hurry.

The task; the sentences are self evident, then writers were told to write the words 'the' and 'running' at increasing speed.

These examples came from a group of fifty teachers at a handwriting conference. The task was designed to give them an understanding of the variability of written letters through their own handwriting. The word 'the' and the letter string 'ing' were analysed for instances of alteration of movement at speed.

In 11 cases (22%) the writer altered to a crossbar join at speed.

In 24 cases (48%) the writer altered the 'g' at speed.

This is a typical case. The writer altered both the join from 't-h' and the 'n-g' at the third instance, when speeding up her writing.

In 28 cases (56%) a baseline join from t-h was used throughout. In 18 cases (36%) a conventional 'g' was retained throughout.

In 11 cases (22%) crossbar joins were used

In 8 cases (16%) a shortcut for the letter 'g' was used throughout.

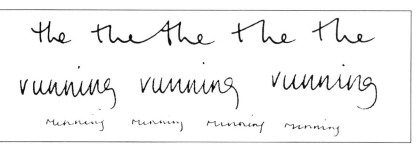

Some teachers had discovered the most efficient forms and employed them, usually without realising it, all the time in their personal handwriting.

When writers see that they themselves alter the movement of letters at speed, they can appreciate the value of such personal shortcuts.

The most interesting cases are those who altered to a crossbar join or a shortcut to the letter 'g' at speed. They demonstrate how unconscious is this change of movement within and between letters.

In some cases the crossbar join became more efficient at speed.

This exercise helped teachers to understand and then how to teach personal joins, and to realise that such shortcuts can be efficient without any appreciable loss of legibility.

In one case the letter 'g' became more intricate at speed.

closed form of the letter produced a straight form in their work. This often showed as different forms in different positions in the word 'kicked', and perhaps suggests that the closed form is not always the most efficient.

Another interesting finding was the frequent appearance of a form of 'k' that is never taught. This two stroke form, illustrated here, makes a lot of sense developmentally. It never requires a young child to commence a stroke in space. It only requires a change of direction plus a final stroke anchored to the upward diagonal. It develops satisfactorily into several efficient retracing forms of 'k'. At the risk of overstating my case, I take this as yet another example of the way inventive children signal their ability to develop more efficient, appropriate and perfectly legible forms of certain letters than they are ever taught in class.

There is just one further aspect of this work to report on. This concerns the use of simple word tests that can illustrate the efficiency of personal variations to an audience of any age.

The easiest of these tests is to ask any writer or group of writers

This form of the letter 'k' might be easier for young children. It develops into several efficient retrace forms. The two examples below were found in the survey.

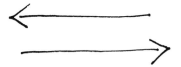

A right-to-left line is easier for most left handers to draw or write.

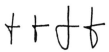

It may be easier to retrace the crossbar stroke before joining.

Some left-handers find ingenious ways of dealing with crossbars.

This nine-year-old left-hander found a most efficient form. She wrote the crossbar first. This worked best when the letter 't' was in the initial position in the word.

Examples of 'woven' and 'vowel' taken from the writing of some of the teachers whose work appears on pages 56 and 57.

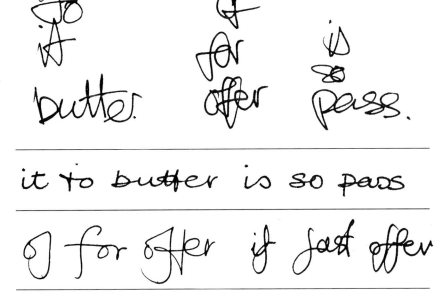

These are the kind of exercises that demonstrate to the writers - preferably teachers or those involved in educational planning - how variable their own handwriting is. The words 'woven' and 'vowel' show how the letters 'v' and 'w' are sometimes spiky and sometimes round, varying between and within words in most adult handwriting. This should lead to an understanding that, after the early stages, children should not be too closely confined to inflexible models. A variable handwriting is fast and usually efficient and such personal variations seldom affect legibility.

These sequences have been used to show students the variability of such letters as 'f', 't' and 's' in different position in words and, more effectively still, of 'ff', 'tt' and 'ss'.

to write the word 'the' three or four times.The only instruction that should be given is that the writer should increasingly speed up until the word becomes a scribble. It is then a matter of finding out if and when the crossbar join takes over from the conventional baseline join. Another useful sequence that illustrates the same point is 'ing'.

To illustrate any personal variations in the forms of letters used within different positions in the word, here are some useful sequences. The words 'if, for and offer', 'is so and pass', or 'it to and butter' usually illustrate the point quite well.

If you want to take this demonstration a stage further, then you can ask participants to change papers and to replicate their neighbour's letterforms. It is particularly difficult to copy another writer's variation of 'ff'.

CHAPTER 4

More about Personal Letters

This paper was presented at the Fourth Conference of the International Graphonomics Society, at the University of Trondheim in 1989. It was subsequently published as Sassoon R (1991), The effects of teachers' personal handwriting on their reproduction of school handwriting models, in *The Development of Graphic Skills*, eds Wann, Wing and Sovik pp 151-62. It is reproduced here by kind permission of Academic Press Ltd.

THE EFFECT OF TEACHERS' PERSONAL HANDWRITING ON THEIR REPRESENTATION OF THE SCHOOL MODEL

In Great Britain there is no nationally prescribed handwriting model. Schools are free to choose whatever letterform model and method of teaching handwriting they wish. When teachers change jobs they may have to learn to demonstrate a completely different handwriting model, both on the blackboard and on paper. This chapter describes two studies concerned with teachers' representations of their schools' handwriting model. It also compares certain details of these representations with the same details as they appear in the teachers' personal handwriting.

In the last decade there have been a number of studies of handwriting models used in British schools. Rubin and Henderson (1982) carried out a questionnaire survey to ascertain which models are most frequently used in schools in certain localities. Brown (1985), in a study of schools in Birmingham, reported that teachers supplement published workbooks with material of their own. She also noted the variety of the writing of children within groups being taught the same system. Sassoon (1988) documented this latter aspect in greater detail, looking at the effects of different models and teaching methods on how children learn to write. This work showed that, although schools may claim to be using a certain handwriting model or scheme, the teachers' reproduction of the model varied considerably, sometimes in essential elements of models. In some cases the whole purpose of the model was negated.

Personal handwriting is seldom consistent in all elements. A scheme for classifying selected sets of handwritten letters was outlined in Eldridge *et al* (1983). This classification presented a measure for summarising the variation within personal handwriting as well as between two writers. Wing *et al* (1983) analysed the variation in letterforms depending on their position in the word, so these studies already detail certain variations in adult cursive handwriting. In this chapter, directed towards educational issues, I take relevant variation and inconsistency to be more concerned with (separate) letters occurring in copy book models, with teachers' representations of such models, with their personal handwriting and with their young pupils' handwriting.

In theory it might be possible to chart all instances of inconsistency between all these scripts occurring in any element and, for example, to measure exactly variations in letter slant, ascender or descender height, or angle of each upstroke. However, the present chapter describes two field studies that were not designed to use any sophisticated measuring equipment. It is part of a body of work that seeks to find simple techniques of analysing letters that may enable teachers and other practitioners in the field of handwriting to use previously written examples for survey and research purposes, and to come to an understanding of the complexity and variability of the written trace. The analysis of letterforms in this study is confined to the level necessary to illuminate specific points about those elements where teachers deviate when reproducing a handwriting model and where these deviations might be connected with their personal handwriting.

Study 1: Teachers' handwriting

Study 1 was part of a larger investigation that looked in detail at the teaching of handwriting in six schools in the southeast of England, reported in Sassoon (1988). The details of the handwriting models used in each school were known (see Figure 1 for an example). It was therefore possible to make comparisons between elements of the teachers' personal letters and the way they reproduced the school model in relation to the same elements of the supposedly taught model. It was also possible to look at specific deviations from the model on the part of some of the teachers and how these deviations affected some of their pupils.

Method

Six schools were chosen because they had used, over a period of years, a particular model or method. In each school, three teachers

Figure 1
One of the models, a modification of Marion Richardson's letters, separated into elements allowing comparison between details of the original model and teachers' representation of it.

elements	model	teacher 1	teacher 2	teacher 3
slant	h k	hill	hill	hill
proportion	O	oo	oo	oo
ascenders	j g b	ball	ball	ball
descenders		ing	ing	ing
crossbar	tur	tath	tath	tath
entry	m r	us	is	is
exit	a w	thiw	thinw	thinw
arches	n u	n u	n u	n u
'e'	e	he	he	he
'b' and 'p'	b p	b p	b p	b p

were tested; the teacher responsible for the handwriting policy of the school (who in three out of the six schools was the head teacher), and the two teachers directly responsible for the classes of seven- and nine-year old pupils who also took part in this investigation. Each teacher was interviewed separately. They were asked to write out the same sentences as their pupils, first in their personal handwriting and then in the model they would use in the classroom.

This allowed two comparisons to be made:

1 Between each school's model and the teachers' representation of it.
2 Between the repesentation of the model and each teacher's personal handwriting.

The purpose of these comparisons was to see whether a personal deviation, linked to the personal handwriting, can affect how a teacher represents the school model. In this abbreviated description, only one element, the slant of the teachers' handwriting, is reported. For complete details the reader should refer to Sassoon (1988).

Results

Overall it was found that the slant of the teachers' reproduction of the model was in every case the same as that of their personal handwriting. Of the 18 possible teachers, one was omitted as she had just joined her school and was still teaching upright print script instead of the forward slanting italic model. In the school where the emphasis was more on method than model (based on Sassoon 1983) the slant of the taught letters corresponded with the teachers' personal handwriting, one forward, one upright and one variable. The formal models in the other five schools all had a slight forward slant. Of the personal handwriting and the reproduction of the model by the fourteen remaining teachers, seven slanted forward and seven did not. Of these, five teachers had an upright handwriting and two showed a backward slant.

Study 2: Rating similarity of handwriting samples

In the second study, examples of teachers' personal handwriting and their reproduction of school models were obtained during in-service courses on the teaching of handwriting held in various centres throughout Great Britain. When comparing two sets of examples of handwriting it is first necessary to decide which of the many elements of strokes or letters to take into consideration. Elements of adults' personal handwriting are likely to be more difficult to analyse than separate letters. It was decided to concentrate initially on only three aspects:

1 slant
2 proportion of the height of the letter base (*x-height*) to the height of the ascender
3 letter width

At the time of data collection – 1985 – most schools taught print script during the first few years of school. Whether a formal model is in use or not, print script letters are accepted as letters with straight terminals. The proportion of the letters may vary slightly, being round, or sometimes oval, depending on the designer of the handwriting model. Although usually upright, print script models occasionally have a forward slant.

Method

To obtain the examples teachers were asked, with no explanations, to 'take down' three sentences. These were the same sentences used for both children and teachers in the six primary schools where the first study took place. The next instruction that the teachers were given was: 'Now write the same sentences in the model that you teach the children in your class at school.' In this way over 200 examples were obtained.

Of the original examples, some had to be discarded because they were incomplete. Others were omitted because they were in cursive or semi-cursive writing which, without exact information about the model in use, would have made any detailed comparison difficult. With these losses 110 examples of representations of print script models were left.

Scoring

The examples were first carefully marked by the author, taking a considerable time to make some of the decisions, finding that the comparison between the widths of letters to be the most difficult to make. Two independent markers, who were not specialists in letterforms, were also enlisted:

1 AT, a retired secondary school teacher
2 MM, a housewife with two school-age children

The markers were asked to make quick visual judgements. They were required to judge whether each of the three elements was similar or dissimilar in each pair of samples. Three suggestions were offered to assist the markers in their judgements:

1 that a ruler and set square could be used in any cases where they were uncertain about the slant of letters
2 that where there was doubt about the proportion of base to ascender height, ruled pencil lines could be made along the lines of writing to assist in the judgement
3 where there was doubt about the proportions of letters then the judgement should be concentrated on the letters 'n' and 'o'. Both markers reported that the task took them about one hour to complete.

Results
Similarities and dissimilarities in slant and proportion
In 68 cases out of 110 (62%), the three markers agreed that all three elements were similar in the teachers' personal writing and in the versions of the school model used by the teachers. The author found 290 elements of similarity overall and 40 elements of dissimilarity. AT found 279 elements of similarity and 51 elements of dissimilarity. MM found 312 elements of similarity and 18 of dissimilarity. Table 1 shows the divergence in the three markers' scores.

Marker	Slant		Ascender		Width	
	S	D	S	D	S	D
RS	78	32	107	3	106	4
AT	78	32	103	7	98	12
MM	98	12	107	3	107	3

The 68 cases in which all elements in the teachers' personal writing were judged by all three markers to be similar to their representation of their models provided the starting point for the next anlaysis.

No definite conclusions could be reached by comparing the proportions of the teachers' writing and that of a print script model because proportions are free to vary in print script models. However, models are more specific in the matter of slant. Some are upright, some have a slight forward slant, but none slant backwards. It was decided to exclude all examples where the slant of the writing was upright or forward as there was no way of knowing whether those teachers might have used an upright or a forward slanting model. This left 28 examples from the original sample of 110. All of these examples slanted backwards in both the teachers' personal handwriting and their representation of print script (see Figure 2). All three markers had been unanimous in their judgement of the similarity of these two points. There are no models in general use in Great Britain that slope backwards. A backward sloping reproduction of a model must threfore be a personal deviation. Where this coincides with a backward slant in the teachers' personal handwriting this is strong evidence that the reproduction of a model can be infuenced by the slant of the writer's hand.

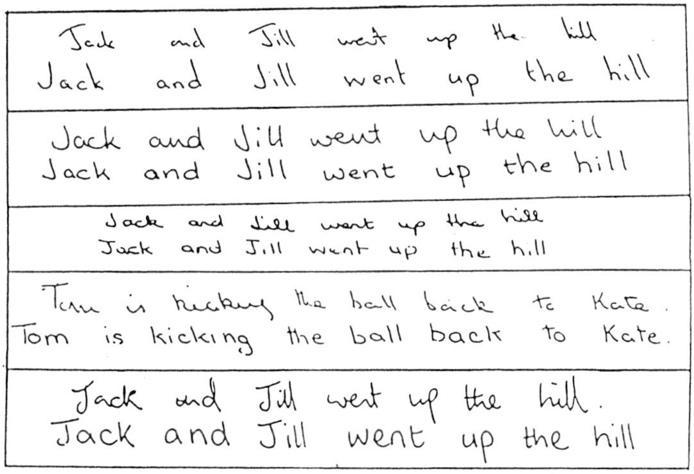

Figure 2
Five examples out of the 28 where the backward slant of the teachers' personal handwriting was repeated in their print script - the model taught to their pupils.

Further points of similarity

The similarity in the point of entry of some teachers' personal handwriting and their representation of print script may be observed in Figure 3. Some print script models demonstrate a top right entry into the letter 'o' some a central entry, but none recommend a top left entry. Five examples are illustrated to demonstrate how teachers used their own top left point of entry to the letter 'o' when reproducing the school model. The examples

top right   central   top left

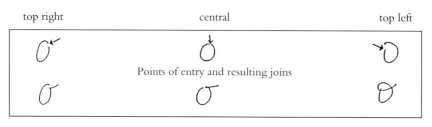

Points of entry and resulting joins

1. Hooton (1983).   2. Barnard (1979).   3. Jarman (1982).

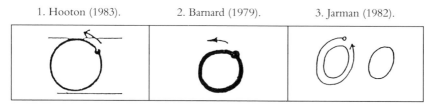

Figure 3
Points of entry and resulting joins. The point of entry to the letter 'o' is usually indicated at the top right for children. Sometimes it is central but never top left.

Examples of the way copybooks indicate the entry to the letter 'o' from: Hooton, Barnard and Jarman.

The five most obvious examples of teachers replicating their own top left point of entry when demonstrating print script.

that are illustrated are the most obvious. Several others showed the same deviation to a lesser extent.

Two other comparisons were made. The first of these concerned the formation of the letter 'b'. This showed that out of the 26 teachers with an undercurve 'b' in their personal handwriting, only one (and this could have been explained by the school model) failed to change the formation of their personal undercurve 'b' to the print script form. The second additional comparison was based on the fact that eight teachers volunteered the information that they used a certain popular commercial handwriting scheme. This allowed some comparisons to be made against the published

Figure 4
The unusual formation of the letter 'k' in a teacher's handwriting (top) also seen reflected in the handwriting of two of her pupils.

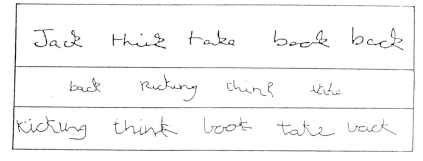

model. Even with this small and unsolicited sample it was possible to note personal deviations from the well-known model that tied up with elements in the teachers' personal handwriting. These deviations included the terminal and also the crossbar of the letter 't', the formation of the letter 'k' (see Figure 4), the length of ascending and descending strokes, and the slant of letters.

Discussion

This study brings out a number of points deserving further investigation. The first point to note is that the findings reported in this paper have been largely confined to the slant of letters. This element may be relatively easy to measure, but may not be the most important factor in influencing the way children learn to write. It might be asked what other deviations occur in teachers' reproduction of models, that, copied by pupils, cause lasting problems in the latter's handwriting?

Another question that might profit from serious research is how do individuals view their own handwriting, and how do they perceive or judge the writing of others? In this study, there was considerable variability in the judgements of letter slant by those who were not specialists in letterforms. It would be interesting to understand factors contributing to such judgements.

Where teachers find it difficult to reproduce a model, it might be asked whether their deviations arise only from habits in their own writing or, additionally, whether they are unable to perceive the different elements of a model? Why, for instance, do many teachers exaggerate some elements such as the triangularity of italic letters as well as misjudging the proportions of letters and the slant which are the important features of certain well-known models? These deviations are reported in detail in Sassoon (1988), but that investigation did not extend to looking, other than anecdotally, at any possible causes other than those posed by personal handwriting habits.

There are implications for educational planning in the findings reported in the present work. The difficulties that teachers have in reproducing models might suggest that there should be less reliance on a strict model and more on a method. Such a method would be based on an understanding of what is essential for the acquisition of an efficient handwriting. Initially this would stress such matters as the point of entry and direction of stroke that would ensure the correct movement of basic letters. As long as they are consistent within a pupil's handwriting, such matters as slant and proportion of letters might be better left to the individual choice.

In many countries, however, it is still considered that the model is the most important part of a handwriting policy. Certain states and countries alter their model periodically in search of the ideal that will provide pupils with good handwriting. Considerable emphasis is put on the adherence to the slant, proportion and other details of such models in the classroom. The children have to work at reproducing close replicas of the model letters at the expense of automating a natural hand.

Another point that merits consideration is the plight of children in a mobile society. They often have to move to other localities and may be forced to change certain aspects of their handwriting to conform with a new school, state or even national policy. Once they have automated a certain slant or proportion of letter, or certain personal details, it is likely (and individual cases are frequently brought to my attention) that they will encounter similar difficulties to that of their teachers when faced by a new model. Perhaps, in the future, a focus on method rather than model might circumvent this difficulty.

Teacher 2, in the school whose model is displayed opposite, misinterpreted the entry in the italic model, following the top left entry in her personal handwriting.

Several of her pupils followed and produced some extraordinary movements within their letters.

A somewhat dated Italic model (Worthy 1954), used in one of the schools, separated into elements allowing comparison of the three teachers representation of it.

This seems a difficult model for teachers to reproduce. Only the first teacher captured some of its characteristics. The confusion that might arise by misinterpreting such a model is illustrated opposite and below.

elements	model	teacher 1	teacher 2	teacher 3
slant	*k l k l*	*hill*	*hill*	*hill*
proportion	*O O*	*oo*	*oo*	*oo*
ascenders	*h j h j*	*ill*	*hill*	*hill*
descenders		*yo*	*up*	*up ay*
crossbar	*t u t u*	*to*	*to*	*to the*
entry	*n i m n*	*in*	*ill in*	*ill is*
exit	*a m i a*	*an*	*an*	*an.*
arches	*n u n u*	*n u*	*in ou*	*an uo in ou*
'e'	*ℓ ℓ*	*e*	*e*	*he te*
triangular letters	*y g y d*	*a c*	*ay go*	

The letter 'e' was written three different ways by the three teachers who were tested.

model	teacher 1	teacher 2	teacher 3
ℓ	*e e*	*e e*	*he ℓ*

MORE ABOUT THE REPRODUCTION OF SCHOOL MODELS

Much of the impact of such work is in the accompanying illustrative material. It was not possible to reproduce all of the relevant illustrations in the published paper so I am pleased to have the opportunity to display more of them here. This gives a wider view of how the teachers are either ignoring some of the vital proportions and details of the models they are supposed to be teaching – or are totally unaware of these elements. All the schools were chosen because they had definite models and had taught these models consistently over a period of years. They all claimed to have trained their teachers to demonstrate the said models, indeed one head (of School 4) defied me to find anything wrong with his teachers' representation of the model.

The findings from this analysis allied with the discrepancies found in the judgements of two people who assisted me in checking the slant and proportion of the letters in many of the examples leads me to believe that it may be very diffcult for those untrained in letterforms to detect even such obvious details as slant.

The movement problems illustrated in the paper show how much influence a teacher's personal hand may have on his or her pupils. I would not like this work to be used to prove how essential it is to have a school model. On the contrary I would use it to demonstrate the necessity to teach the essentials of our writing system, in particular the movement of basic letters. Beyond that, it might help adults to understand that if they cannot perceive and produce the elements of a model exactly, then why should they expect children to be able to do so. Variation of slant and proportion and certain other details of letters should not only be tolerated but understood and even encouraged. Where a teacher has personal idiosyncrasies that he or she is unable to eradicate when writing on the blackboard or elsewhere, then this too could be recognised, and the disadvantages or otherwise of copying them discussed with the class. This could also help all concerned to understand how motor patterns, such as those encountered in handwriting, are diffcult to change once they are established.

This section includes extra unpublished material from Sassoon (1988) to illustrate how teachers' reproduction of school models vary, sometimes to the detriment of their pupils.

The Ruth Fagg (1962) model, used in another of the schools, separated into elements allowing comparison between three teachers' representation of it.

elements	model	teacher 1	teacher 2	teacher 3
slant	*l h k*	hill.	hill	hill
proportion	*O*	♂♂	o o	◦◦
ascenders	*b p*	ball	ba ll	ball
descenders		youp	upay	ngp
crossbar	*t u*	the to	th to	thto
entry	*n r i u*	is in	is in	in
exit	*t l t ll*	hill in	hill	ill
arches	*n u*	r u	r u	n u
'e'	*e*	the	he we	he

Teacher 2 exaggerated the exit strokes into a zig zag. Many of the seven-year-old pupils copied her rather than the model. The influence was still visible in the writing of nine-year olds who, two years previously, had been taught by the same teacher.

model	teacher 3	seven-year-olds	nine-year-olds

elements	model	teacher 1	teacher 2	teacher 3
slant	*h k*	Jill	Jill	Jill
proportion	*o*	oo	oo	oo
ascenders	*pg d*	hill	hill	hill
descenders		ing	ing	ing
crossbar	*tw*	to the	to the	to th
entry	*m r*	in	in	in
exit	*a w*	thin	thin	thin
arches	*n u*	n u	n u	n u
'e'	*e*	te	te	te
'b' and 'p'	*b p*	b p	b p	b p

A second school in the survey used the Marion Richardson model. An analysis of teachers' representation of its elements is shown here to show that misinterpretations are not confined to an isolated case.

It is interesting to note that the teacher whose representation most closely resembled the model (teacher 3) had herself attended the same school and had been taught the same model. It can be assumed that, a generation earlier, more attention was paid to the teaching of handwriting and closer attention to the following of the model, and that such training might have had some lasting effect.

CHAPTER 5

Children's Signatures

Introduction

This chapter on children's signatures could be viewed as another extension of the study of variability of personal letters under different speeds and when engaged in different tasks. A great deal has been published on the subject of adult signatures but little attention has been paid to children. There was no particular end in mind when I decided to include a signature-writing task initially for the 15+ group. Children possess bank books and other documents that require the verification of a signature at ever earlier ages, so maybe the study could be helpful in that direction. I soon realised, however, that a differently designed project would have been needed to test the consistency of young people's signatures.

My main concern was to obtain as natural and unstudied example of each pupil's signature as possible. The layout of my test task was appropriate for this. School children are accustomed to being asked to write their name at the top of a sheet of work. The written tasks involved took perhaps five to ten minutes, so there would be a distinct separation of time and attention between the act of name writing and of signature writing. To the unsuspecting pupils it was not so unexpected to be asked to sign their name at the end of a piece of work. If anyone asked why, they were given the answer that it was to make sure it was all their own work. Most of the pupils responded well to being asked to repeat their signature, although a few became so intoxicated by the idea that they could not be stopped from further experimentation. A further sample of fifty boys and fifty girls aged 13+ were tested in the same two schools, at a later date, for comparisons of their written samples. It was not possible to go through the time-comsuming procedure of individual testing and photographing that took place with the older group. It was only the left-handers that were tested individually in the younger group. This was because of my discovery of the interesting postural changes that were detected in some of the older left-handers and reported in the following paper.

THE DEVELOPMENT OF CHILDREN'S SIGNATURES

This paper was presented at the Fifth Conference of the International Graphonomics Society in Tempe, Arizona in 1991. It was delivered to a particularly full and interested multi-disciplinary audience, but was not considered for publication in the usual book of selected papers owing to the imminent publication of this volume.

This study observes development of children's signatures and looks at the differences between the way children write their names and sign them. There are several questions to be addressed in such a project:

1 Are children aware of what a signature is? If so how do they perceive their signature, and how do their concepts of a signature develop over the teenage years?
2 How consistent are they likely to be in repeating a signature and what, if any, circumstances contribute to the maturing of a signature?

A signature is isolated. It is not part of what has been written before, nor a part of anything that is to come, so it is likely to develop as a personal hieroglyph presenting the writers and their character to the world. Jacoby (1938) calls the signature 'the psychological visiting card of a person'. Roman (1952) states that 'Even the young child has need of such visible representation of himself. . . thus the foundation for the ultimate pattern of his signature is laid'. Saudek (1932), though not specifically referring to signatures, compares children's handwriting to adults '. . . It even offers possibilities absent from maturer specimens. From the latter we are able to observe what a man is. From a child's handwriting, on the other hand, can often be seen what he is likely to become.'

It is useful to start by defining some of the differences that are likely to occur between signatures and name writing or ordinary handwriting:

1 Speed is likely to influence the letters and pressures, slant and individuality of the letterforms in signatures.
2 Stresses on certain features such as capital letters are likely to develop as well as simplifications of other letters which might not be typical of the writer's ordinary handwriting.
3 Different usage of full names or initials are likely to occur.

Method
Great care was taken to ensure that relaxed examples were gathered. This was done by working with pupils in their school environment and by separating the two acts of name writing and signing. It is usual in a school situation to request that the name should be written at the top of the page before commencing work. An unrelated handwritten task lasting about ten minutes was then set and undertaken. At the end of the task the pupils were asked to write their signature. Those who asked what a signature was were told to sign their name to show that the writing had been their own work. They were then asked to repeat their signature as a check for consistency in their signature writing. Fifty girls and fifty boys in each of the third and fifth year of secondary schooling, a total of 200 children, were involved. Whole sets of children were used to eliminate any teacher choice in the matter so a few twelve-year-olds were caught in the third year sample which was taken at the beginning of a school year. The older group was tested later in the school year, and each pupil was tested individually and photographed while in the act of writing. This proved time-consuming but useful in that it pinpointed the few pupils in that group who had markedly different writing strategies for signature writing.

Classifications
Comparisons between name writing and signatures
The first analysis would differentiate only between two issues:
   1 Similar in all points
   2 Dissimilar in one or all points

Dissimilarities between namewriting and signature
Then the various differences could be tabulated:
   1 Differences in presentation; full name or initials
   2 Difference in slant
   3 Difference in size
   4 Difference in layout or alignment
   5 Difference usage of capital letters or small letters
   6 Different forms of capital or small letters
   7 Difference in the amount of joining
   8 Difference in spacing of words or letters

9   Flourishes, underlining or encircling
10 Difference in punctuation
11 Noticeable simplification of letters
12 Difference in writing stategies

Many of the classifications could be subdivided to reveal more details, and, as this is an open-ended analysis, future examples may reveal features that require additional points to be added.

Comparison between two examples of signatures
The first analysis would differentiate only between:
1   Similar in all points
2   Dissimilar in one or more points

More detailed analyses could be undertaken using as many of the twelve listed dissimilarities as were appropriate to any particular sample.

Findings

A consistently high proportion of children demonstrated slight differences between their name writing and their signature as would be expected:

At 12/13 years 87%: (43 boys out of 50, 44 girls out of 50)
At 15/16 years 85%: (42 boys out of 50, 43 girls out of 50)

When examined in more detail a considerable decrease in the dissimilarities could be perceived with age in certain categories. The most frequently occurring differences overall were:

Difference in presentation of full name or initials:
at 12/13: 53%   at 15/16: 39%   46% overall

Difference in joining:
at 12/13: 54%   at 15/16: 36%   45% overall

Difference in slant:
at 12/13: 51%   at 15/16: 31%   41% overall

Differences in flourishing, underlining or encircling:
at 12/13: 56%   at 15/16: 22%   39% overall

Difference in letterforms:		
at 12/13: 31%	at 15/16: 33%	32% overall

Differences in size:		
at 12/13: 30%	at 15/16: 23%	26.5% overall

A different way of grouping categories together could provide a clearer interpretation of the findings. If the three first categories – difference in presentation – joining and slant are grouped together, they represent an average of 52.67% of 12/13 year olds and 35.33% of those at 15+. The decrease of these particular differences in dissimilarities with age is likely to be caused by the maturing of the pupils' handwriting. The decrease in flourishing, in particular, most likely indicates a maturing of the signature. The differences in letterforms and size are not so marked and require further analysis to show whether the alterations in individual cases are more or less mature in relation to the name writing.

It is the very personal nature of handwriting, in this case as a measure of maturity, that makes statistical analysis of such material so complex. The illustrations show the full range from mature twelve-year-old signatures which indicate that they have already been developed and practised over a period of time, to pupils at 15+ who have not yet developed a signature that is dissimilar to their immature name writing

The only noticeable boy/girl differences were:

	Layout and alignment		
	12/13 15%	15+ 10%	
	comprising		
Boys:	at 12/13 10%	at 15+	10%
Girls:	at 12/13 5%	at 15+	5%

	Punctuation		
	12/13 22%	15+ 34%	
	comprising		
Boys:	at 12/13 6%	at 15+	8%
Girls:	at 12/13 16%	at 15+	26%

Neither the issues involved nor the number of pupils make these dissimilarities as important as those above which involved the whole sample.

Dissimilarities between two examples of signatures

The comparison between two examples of signatures was confined to the older sample who were individually supervised to make sure that they complied with the instructions. Only 42% of the younger children complied with the instructions. The others either gave only one signature or covered a considerable area of the page with experiments.

Within the older group 36 boys and 27 girls showed no discernable differences between the two signatures. Where there were dissimilarities with a few exceptions they were minor. For example, 18 of them were provided by differences in punctuation or dots on 'i'. With very few exceptions (see illustration) the differences were so minor that they demonstrated that this method was probably not appropriate for gathering information about the consistency of signatures. It would be better to test on separate occasions and maybe in different environments if such information is required.

Discussion

This study was meant to be a relatively quick visual means of comparing signatures and name writing without using the computer-linked equipment that would provide such information as differences in writing pressure and accurate comparisons of speed. This work has the merit, however, of recording material that has been gathered in natural surroundings and, as nearly as possible, relates to automatically written work rather than the more conscious examples that may result from testing in laboratory situations. A longitudinal study would be needed to record development within individuals, and to question more intensively attitudes and circumstances that may have influenced certain features of the developing signature. However, great care would be needed to ensure natural rather than conscious or forced examples of signatures.

The findings show that there is usually a decrease in dissimilarities with age, and they indicate where the majority of the

Figure 1
Some of the younger group appeared to view the signature as an opportunity for excessive size and embellishment.

dissimilarities lie. It is the illustrations, however, rather than the statistics that provide most information about the developmant of signatures, and they deserve further interpretation. They illustrate, for example, the sometimes artificial and exaggerated flourishes of a few of the younger children who may see a signature just as an embellishment of their name. In some cases it is enough to compare the name with the signature, but in other cases the written tasks provide the vital links. The tasks included both ordinary speed text writing, and fast writing. Details of the tasks can be found in Sassoon, Wing and Nimmo-Smith (1989), along with some of the detailed differences between the fast and slow writing of this same sample.

The name writing of some of the less mature of the younger pupils shows faults of incorrect capital letter usage and poorly formed letters that do not appear in the text writing. This may be explained by the fact that children automate their name writing at a young age and in some cases fail to upgrade it as their other handwriting matures. In other words, the name writing may lag

Paul King

Pauline Richards.

Kelly Burton

Figure 2
For some children the
perception of a
signature seemed to be
not so much a flourish,
but crossings-out,
defacing the name.

behind the level of ordinary classroom writing. The signature,
even at 12/13 however, usually shows more maturity than the text
writing, although in isolated places the maturer and faster
elements that appear in the signature may already be seen if the
texts are scrutinised. This suggests that the signature allows an
opportunity for the pupil to experiment and to escape from the
school imposed model.

When two years later most of the everyday handwriting has
matured, the differences between many of the elements of name
and signature may be reduced. Then the mature elements of the
signature may be signalling what the pupil is about to become.

Once sufficiently practised and stabilised, the signature may be
reduced to more of a personalised monogram. As consistency is
more necessary than legibility in a signature, this is not necessarily
a disadvantage. From the sample there was only one signature that
could be termed undecipherable. On questioning, the writer, a
fifteen-year-old boy, replied that he had developed it because he
had a 'Saturday job' in a warehouse that necessitated his constantly
signing for deliveries of merchandise. This raises the point that
mature signatures may develop partly from usage. The converse is
that some children may not develop fast simplifed signatures
without the need to use them.

A totally unrelated finding arose from observing the writers

	Name writing	Signature

Figure 3
The range in maturity of the signatures in the lower age range was extensive. These examples of 12/13 year old pupils suggest that many of them had established and practised their signatures. Some of them had designed their signatures using similar letterforms to those in their name writing while others used letters that did not yet appear even in her fast writing.

Name and slow writing	Signature and fast writing	Figure 4

Figure 5
Several pupils in the older group had simplified their letters to a stage where they were not easily decipherable. The most simplified example, no. 3, came from a boy who had consciously developed his economical signature as a result of having a Saturday job that requires frequent signing of his name.

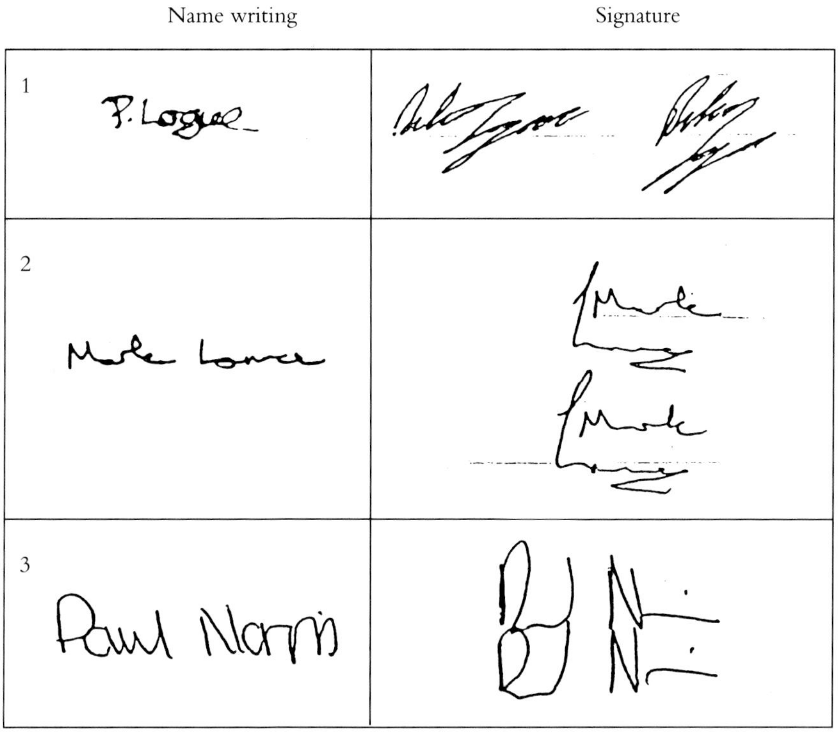

	Name writing	Signature
1		
2		
3		

while performing the writing of their names and signatures. It was noted in the cases of two left-handed girls (out of 7 in the 15+ sample) and one left-handed boy (out of 8 in the sample) that they altered writing strategies between the two tasks. All three changed from non-inverted to inverted posture to write their signature. In all three cases the writers also altered their paper position. They were asked three times each to perform the two tasks and made the same alterations each time, being photographed while they did so. It was an unconscious act on the part of all three. None of the writers was aware of what he or she had done, and initially offered no explanation. When questioned more closely all three were initially surprised at this occurrence, but then reported that they had altered from the inverted position to the non-inverted when they had to speed up their handwriting in secondary school. None of them could accurately pinpoint the date when this had occurred. This suggests that they had automated their signature before altering their penhold and reverted to inverting only for this

Name writing	Signature
1	
2	
3	
4	
5	
6	

Figure 6
Some examples showed dissimilarities between usage of capital letters within names and signatures. In nos. 1 and 4, this might be explained by the way some children automate their names at an early age, often coming to school writing in capital letters, and fail to alter them. No. 5 still mixed the usage of capital letters in his text. Other pupils might be influenced by the instructions found on most forms which ask for 'block letters'. Cases such as nos. 5 and 6 cannot easily be explained.

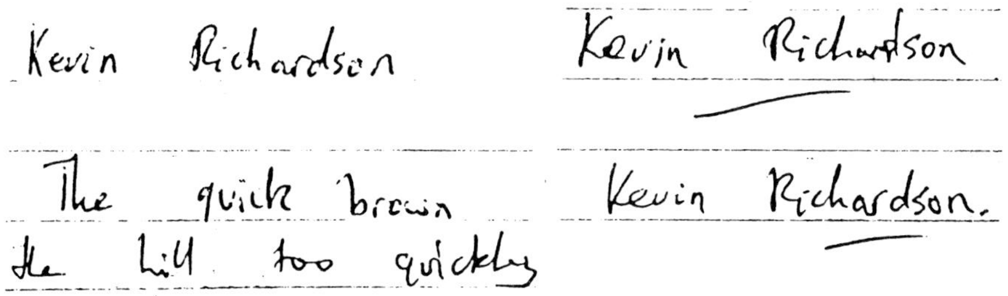

Figure 7
The decrease in dissimilarities with age may be accounted for by the maturing of the handwriting of the students. This pupil showed a mature handwriting for a fifteen-year-old, with little difference betwen name writing and signature except for the underlining.

Kevin Richardson   Kevin Richardson

The quick brown   Kevin Richardson.
the hill too quickly

purpose. The illustrations are accurately drawn from the photographs and the signatures are reproduced to show the alteration in proportion and slant that resulted from the altered writing strategies.

In addition to any information about the development of a signature these findings add an interesting observation to the arguments concerning left-handers' hand positions. These three pupils seem to suggest that some writers can move from inverted to non-inverted at will with no contra-indications as might be suggested from the research of Levy and Reid (1978) whose hypothesis is that persons who write using the inverted posture have ipsilateral control of distal limb movement. Nor need the distinction between inverters and non-inverters be as clear cut as the work of Athene and Guiard (1991) suggests. It has been my contention, as discussed in chapter 8, that care should be taken over the implications of findings of classroom observations that quantify certain features, such as the aforementioned paper on left-handed inverters. Not only should the effects of any postural training be taken into account but it would now seem that, left to themselves, some children are capable of altering as they find an inverted position inhibits the speed of writing. This has long been my contention from observation and treatment of children and adults with handwriting problems in a medical environment in

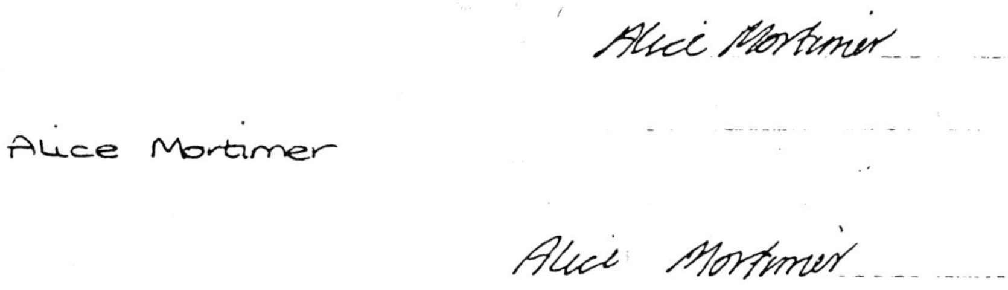

Figure 8
Alice Mortimer, like the two left-handers on the following page, altered hand and paper position between name or text writing and writing her signature.

Alice Mortimer

Alice Mortimer

Alice Mortimer

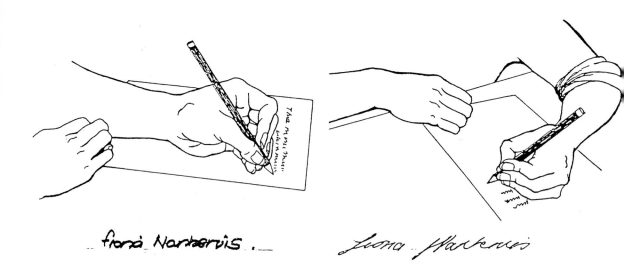

particular. Many such persons have quite easily altered their hand posture when it caused them pain or discomfort, once it was explained to them that first a change of paper position was required. Sassoon (1990) in particular stresses the interaction between paper position, hand position and penhold – and of course the resulting written trace.

Observing how these three pupils all altered their paper position automatically between name writing and signature signalled a welcome affirmation of this concept. It raises the educational point that this suggestion should be put with more confidence to those who appear to be inhibited by an inverted position, while not

Figures 9a and 9b
Three of the fifteen-year-old left-handers (out of 15) used different strategies for name writing and signatures. Their hand was non-inverted for name and text writing but was inverted for signature writing. The paper position was also altered between tasks.

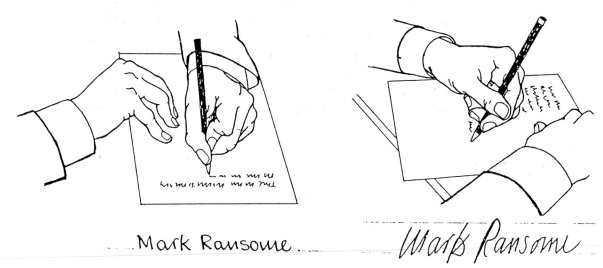

interfering with those who find it an acceptable and pain-free strategy. What it has to say about signature writing in particular is less clear. It reinforces, however, the concept that, once automated, any aspect of handwriting becomes so spontaneous that the writer is often unconscious of the act, however bizarre or even painful the position or unusual the procedure that results in the written trace.

Conclusion

This particular mix of tasks reveals a rich source for further study, not only in the development of signatures but also into letterform variation.

There is also an educational perspective. The extra maturity of many of the signatures suggests perhaps the talents and characteristics of each – whereas the comparative immaturity of much of the name and text writing suggests the inhibiting influence of imposed school models and the expectation of conformity from peer group and social pressures within the classroom.

Two important issues are introduced: comparisons between the writing of twins, and the way that some left-handers alter writing posture and paper position between tasks. This shows that teenagers can alter their hand position spontaneously from an awkward inverted posture to a non-inverted one if the act of writing is painful or slow.

MORE ABOUT SIGNATURES

A presentation to the International Graphonomics Society requires a certain amount of statistical analysis or evidence, therefore I complied with this requirement. Personally I do not attach a great deal of importance to the analyses of the differences between names and signatures in this sample, and even less to the very minor difference that were found by comparing two examples of individuals' signatures. They seem only to confirm commonsense judgements that could have been reached quite easily without them. This does not mean that I do not believe this work to be of importance in other ways. As so often in my work, the visual arrangements of material are as forceful, if not more so, than the statistics.

A great deal more work is left to do on this fascinating set of examples. For instance, a more detailed comparison of the name writing and signatures of the three sets of identical twins in itself

Left-handed twin   Right-handed twin

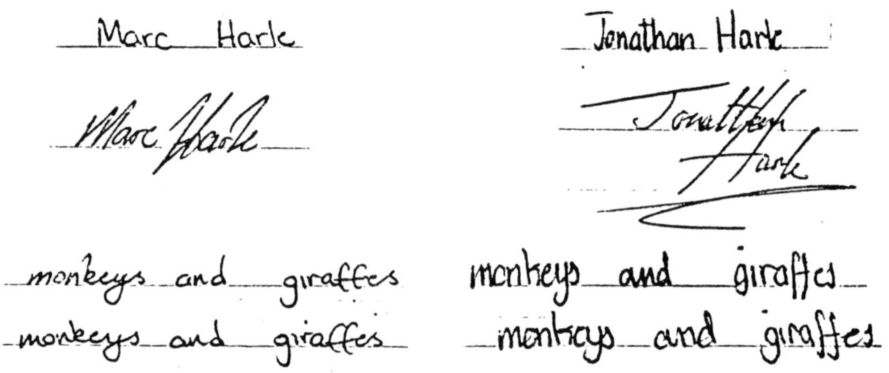

Figure 10
There were three sets of identical twins in the sample. Two were mirror-image twins comprising a left-hander and a right-hander, while the third pair consisted of two right-handers. In all three cases the signature showed marked similarities, whereas in the ordinary handwriting the dissimilarities were more noticeable, in particular the letters 'k' and 'f'.

would be rewarding. All of them could be traced for follow-up examples now, several years later.

For me, however, by far the most important finding arose from the fact that all the pupils had been individually observed and photographed in the act of writing both the task and, where appropriate, the signature. This method disclosed the three left-handers (out of fifteen pupils) who displayed a change of paper and hand position (from non-inverted to inverted) between name

Left-handed twin   Right-handed twin

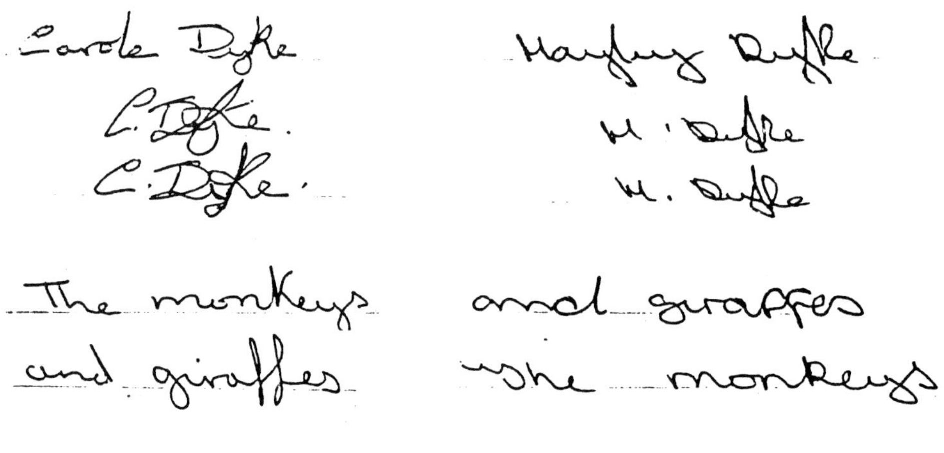

writing and signature writing. Apart from any implications on the development of their signatures, this provided me with the first real evidence that teenagers can spontaneously alter from an inverted hand position at will. Not only had they altered themselves spontaneously but all three were unaware of what they were doing. I regret that I had no video with me, as each of them was asked three times to alternate his or her name and signature, and between each task unconsciously shifted paper, hand and body. I have ample photographic evidence of these occurrences, and for the sake of clarity some of those photographs have been produced as accurate line drawings for this chapter.

The personal repertoire of letters available to these individuals is revealed as a result of the various tasks, fast and slow writing and the even more unself-conscious signature writing. This all deserves wider analysis. Even at a casual glance such variety in efficiency and maturity must indicate how ill-advised is the continued imposition or even expectation of uniform letterforms within personal handwriting – now that the historical necessity for this has passed. It suggests above all how this maturity and efficiency is being inhibited by social, peer group and educational influences and expectations.

The alternative penhold

1 Egyptian scribes from a limestone relief (Saqqara 6th Dynasty)

2 From Callewaert (1962) *Graphologie et Physiologie de L'Ecriture.*

The alternative penhold is beneficial for adults and children alike. It is nothing new, many people find it out for themselves. It is particularly suitable for use with modern pens because they function best when held in a more upright position than a traditional pen or pencil. The use of this penhold for those with severe problems was highlighted by the Belgian neurologist, Callewaert. Throughout history; when writing implements altered so did the prescription for penhold. Modern pens are here to stay, and we need to experiment. If we continue to have an inflexible attitude to penhold, many people will continue to find the act of writing painful.

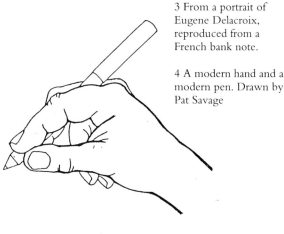

3 From a portrait of Eugene Delacroix, reproduced from a French bank note.

4 A modern hand and a modern pen. Drawn by Pat Savage

CHAPTER 6

An Investigation into Writer's Cramp

The medical aspects of handwriting

Shortly after the publication of my first book on handwriting in 1983 I began to be approached by specialists from several areas of medicine. As my book had been about children's problems, enquiries from those concerned with the medical or psychological care of children was not unexpected. An approach from a neurologist to see his adult patients was more unexpected. I have subsequently been lucky enough, through the interest of psychologists, neurologists, paediatricians, and senior therapists all over the country, to be exposed to a wide variety of patients. It worked this way: there seemed to be no precedent for treating serious handwriting problems, and needless to say, no funding either.

The inability to write did not seem to be considered by many to be in the same category as other daily living skills, as being worthy of serious consideration. Those dealing with severely handicapped children showed considerable ingenuity in devising techniques for wielding a pencil but even so the solutions were, to my mind, still too conventional. Too often they were dependent on expensive commercial aids and did not seem to take into account how flexible writing techniques can be and still succeed. Adults were left with little advice, whether when recovering from a stroke or afflicted with writer's cramp. 'Computers are around; why should anyone worry about handwriting' seemed to be the general feeling. This attitude ignores the fact that anyone who cannot fill in a form or produce a consistent signature is degradingly dependent on someone else for even the most minor transactions.

I decided to treat all this as an extension of my research. In fact several years earlier I had been set the task, by my Cambridge colleagues, of looking at the practical problems of those who had lost the use of their natural writing hand. We never wrote this joint project up, but what I learned in that investigation has proved most valuable. In addition, a presentation on those early findings at an Eastern Motor Group meeting at Addenbrookes Hospital opened a great many doors for future work. Part of what I learned was to recognise and harness the basic human desire to make one's mark. The most damaged hand can make some kind of a mark, and with a bit of imagination this mark can be worked up into a letter. From there it is a short step to name writing. To practise one's name is a positive action – far better than the standard therapeutic practice of transferring buttons from a full box to an empty. Visual feedback allied to the natural motivation to improve the name/signature seemed to lead to much quicker improvement in hand function. I learned another lesson from the best left-handed writer in our local hospital's stroke club. After a year he was indeed very competent with his left hand. I asked him about his supposedly useless right hand and his answer was illuminating. Of course, he explained, he could now write quite well with his right hand, but everyone seemed so delighted with his performance with his left hand that he did not like to disappoint them.

Putting these ideas together seemed to point to writing therapy with the affected hand as soon as possible – and I have fought hard ever since to have name writing included in the list of daily living skills worthy of informed treatment.

In any medical work that I have been asked to undertake I have promised no miracle cures; I have tried to combine clinical sessions with in-service lectures and above all never charged for seeing a patient. I have had only one condition – and even that I have sometimes broken. I will only see patients once, in a diagnostic situation. I am not therapist by nature or training. As a result I have had a strange combination of honorary consultancies and 'arrangements' with various hospitals. It all added up to a fascinating and, in my consideration, a very privileged position, and I am only extremely grateful for those who entrusted their patients to me.

A few difficulties arose when it came time to write up the most pressing of these projects – problems of confidentiality, if nothing else. Problems had already begun to appear with my Writer's Cramp patients who had to be convinced, that despite their neurologists' diagnosis, their condition would respond to commonsense suggestions – sometimes with amazing rapidity. I did not wish to alienate those who had been so helpful to me, and it seemed unlikely that a medical journal would accept my rather general overview of my five years' work with this rather diverse set of patients. I decided to use this paper when I was asked to edit a handwriting volume for the American journal, *Visible Language*. This long-established journal describes itself as concerned with 'research and ideas that help define the unique role and properties of written language'. It reaches a multi-disciplinary readership, but I am glad of an opportunity to reproduce the paper here in a context that may well reach an audience more specifically concerned with handwriting.

This paper was first published in *Visible Language* Volume 22 number 2, (1990), a special issue entitled *The Hand and the Trace, Some Issues in Handwriting,* guest ed. R Sassoon .

WRITER'S CRAMP

Writer's cramp is a controversial area pertaining to handwriting: there is little agreement on the part of the experts. Additionally, there is often little help for the sufferers of this particular condition. This article does not set out to challenge medical views on what is a baffling and increasingly common complaint, but makes a plea for cooperation among the different disciplines involved, in the interests of both patients and research.

This is not the right occasion to present case studies but to give an overview in the form of a distillation from observations of perhaps 50 recent cases of writer's cramp. Individual patients have shown obvious differences in details, but a general pattern of symptoms and attitudes has emerged, along with a pattern of responses to similar suggestions for rehabilitation. A research project is planned to test the long-term implications of this work – not only for the patients but for the attitudes generally held towards the condition of writer's cramp itself. Longitudinal studies are necessary to validate any therapeutic technique, but inevitably they take both considerable time and money. This contribution is offered as an interim document in the hope that it will stimulate discussion and experimentation. It may also give hope to writer's cramp sufferers and should alert any readers to reconsider their writing strategies if they find it painful to wield a pen.

Research review

Writer's cramp is by no means a modern complaint. Solly (1864) reported on 'scrivener's palsy or writer's paralysis'. He stated, 'Upon your early correct diagnosis may depend the health and happiness of your patient. If you mistake its real nature and regard it as incipient softening of the brain, you may destroy the happiness of your patient and bring on the very disease that you have erroneously diagnosed.' Solly described 'how the muscles cease to obey the mandate of the will' and linked scrivener's cramp to the several other occupations where sets of muscles are paralysed by long-continued exertions: shoemaker's cramp, milking cramp, musician's cramp, compositor's and the sempstress' cramp. It is interesting to note that he says of writer's cramp that 'this form of palsy is rare notwithstanding that the greatest part of the middle classes of London get their bread by the use of the pen'. Modern technology may have solved the problems of shoemakers, milkmaids, compositors and sempstresses, but musicians still suffer from cramps, and their symptoms are often compared with those of writers.

Sheehy and Marsden (1982) provide an historical review of the literature on writer's cramp, noting that quite recently it was still being described as 'primarily psychogenic'. They refer to writer's cramp as a focal dystonia and divide it into two categories:

1 Simple writer's cramp – where the patient only exhibits difficulties when writing, other manual acts being carried out normally.
2 Dystonic writer's cramp – where muscle spasms affect not only writing but other manual tasks, such as the ability to handle a knife and fork, cup and saucer, etc.

Hughes and McLellan (1985) put forward an interesting point, saying, 'We suggest that writing is prone to induce dystonia because of concurrent requirements. The first is to hold the pen securely in the fingers and to keep it applied evenly to the paper. The second is to permit rapid and very fine modulation of activity in all the co-activating muscles.' Muscles that oppose one another (flexors and extensors) must be tensed within a conventional tripod grip, and at the same time, delicately controlled to form the letters. This 'conflict' would be exacerbated by the environment in which many people have to write today, at speed and often under considerable tension in competitive situations.

The Belgian neurologist Callewaert (1962, 1962, 1963) held interesting views on the effects of penhold and training on writer's cramp or 'hyperkinesia', as he reported it to have been termed by Jacoub in the last century. Callewaert (1963) suggested that 'indeed such patients have been writing since primary school with exaggerated effort.' He continued, 'It is thus possible to illustrate writer's cramp with a picture of an unskillful child in the handwriting act.' He considered that 'skilled writers' as well as those writing habits have been altered through education, exhibit complete relaxation of those muscles not directly involved in the act of writing'.

In additional to recommendations concerning penhold, Callewaert held strong and somewhat controversial views on letterforms. He considered the extension movements that lead to slanting letters to be difficult. He stated his own point of view that 'handwriting has now evolved to the extent that each letter is formed with an unbroken curved line avoiding interruptions and angles'. While accepting the possibilities of such letters as a therapeutic measure, it may have been this involvement in letterforms that did not conform to the models used in many other countries at that time that prevented Callewaert's work from reaching a wider audience. His 1962 paper was delivered at an international conference on handwriting at the University of Wisconsin. Despite his emphasis on the teaching of handwriting to children, this comment can be found in the discussion following his presentation: 'The author has not presented experimental evidence in support of the round method, and his efforts appear to be primarily clinical. We have to assume that Dr Callewaert's research has been directed toward the age-old student's disease, writer's cramp. The round method then is a system initiated as a therapeutic measure to minimize the tension and discomfort of writing through the relaxation of useless muscles.'

Callewaert's own defence of the round-hand method of writing, with the pen held between the index and middle finger, appeared in an English summary at the end of an article written in French. 'In this technique our two most agile fingers bend their phalanges simultaneously (in order to obtain loops and curves); the combined and harmonious action of the index and middle finger reduces to the minimum the opposition of the thumb which frequently obstructs the writer's movements when the instrument is held in the usual manner. This is in accordance with the view of Hughes and McLellan in obviating the adverse effects of the pad-to-pad opposition of the traditional tripod grip.

Callewaert's work has been helpful to my own clinical observations and in the development of therapeutic techniques. One example of a penhold similar to that recommended by Callewaert was found during the detailed research into penholds leading to Sassoon, Wing and Nimmo-Smith (1986), where the particular advantage of such a grip when using modern pens was discussed. Other such 'alternative' penholds were later found occurring spontaneously in schoolchildren and adults in several different countries, where individuals had found them to their benefit. With the assurance that Callewaert's work provided, that this was unlikely to be harmful to anyone, I was able to proceed with confidence in recommending the particular penhold that he suggested, and other similarly unconventional penholds, to patients.

A personal view of writer's cramp

The first and perhaps main point raised here is whether writer's cramp should be looked at entirely as a medical condition. Neurologists, psychiatrists or surgeons (depending on the referral) will see their patients when they are already already in a serious condition, and must prescribe accordingly. There are aspects of this condition, however, that may be influenced by the specific implications of handwriting itself, as different from the purely mechanical repetitive movement of the muscles. There seems to be a basic need of humans to express themselves in a graphic way. The intellectual involvement in the content of writing and the emotional environment in which the act takes place may all play a part. Above all, the effect of the visible trace itself on the writer – the failure involved in either the total inability to produce a personal mark, or the disintegration of a once adequate writing – needs considering. These aspects could be implicit in the act, stemming initially from handwriting rather than from the nervous system.

By treating patients with the same techniques used for more

general handwriting problems, it is often possible to alleviate the symptoms of patients who have been diagnosed as having writer's cramp. While it is not yet possible to say whether such patients are 'cured'. at least they have had their ability to write restored. In addition, this may be one way that clues to the nature of this complaint may be disclosed.

We can start by considering some possible commonsense, rather than medical, causes of writer's cramp, in particular why this complaint should be on the increase. Modern technology should be alleviating the situation by taking many of the more extensive tasks onto keyboards. We need to explore all aspects of this complex subject. Some clues to the explanation of some symptoms can be found within the historical repertoire of letterforms and penholds; others can be found by examining changing educational methods or while examining the effects of modern writing implements.

Pain

Many writer's cramp patients suggest that the origins of their trouble date back to stressful periods when handwriting became painful for them. The pain appeared to have arisen from a variety of causes and occasionally began quite early in their school days. This study of adult writer's cramp sufferers must be seen as an extension of many years of working with children with handwriting problems. Many of them suffer considerable pain when writing. A small but worrying survey reported in Sassoon (1990) found 40% of girls and 25% of boys of school-leaving age could be counted as suffering pain when writing. This was quantified after they had responded to a six-point diagnostic list that involved the seat of pain, which specific tasks caused most pain, duration of pain, etc. Less formal surveys with higher achieving pupils of the same age pointed to an even higher proportion of pain. Tension tremors can occasionally be observed in children under stress. Such tremors improve or worsen depending on the children's home or school environment.

Occasionally, the pain and tension can be so intense that pupils become unable to use their writing hand. This is often related to overuse at examination time, but cases of younger children appear to be on the increase worldwide, especially in countries where the education system is highly competitive. Can this, then, be termed juvenile writer's cramp?

Handwriting within the educational system

This must bring into question the way that our children are taught to write and the usage of writing within primary, secondary and tertiary education. My own feelings are that writing problems are induced by our educational system, and the ignorance concerning the needs of writers is worsening in many countries as a generation that has not had adequate instruction becomes the teachers of the next, unfortunate generation. In particular:

1   Schools all over the world consider the written trace but seldom the writers – in particular, not their hands or body posture.
2   There is an idea that there is a conventional, and therefore unalterable, right or wrong way of doing things, instead of an understanding that both writing implements and the usage of handwriting have changed dramatically in the last few decades. This might mean that different attitudes to writing strategies are needed.
3   The almost universal insistence on neatness leads to an unbalanced view of the purpose of writing, which can have disastrous results for those who cannot relax this perfectionist standard when educational or other real-life situations demand speed. A more flexible attitude is needed from the start, recognising different levels of writing appropriate for different tasks.

Other contributory causes

The factors listed here as possible contributing causes of writer's cramp can be viewed separately or as an inexorable progression.

1   Unsuitable writing strategies: posture, paper position and above all, penhold that rapidly become habitual. Writers themselves do not seem to realise that quite simple factors are affecting their comfort. They continue to twist their bodies to adapt to some unsuitable paper position instead of just moving the paper. They strain their hands without realising how they are harming themselves when simple experimentation with new, and not necessarily conventional, penholds might provide a solution.

2 Tension and pain when the hand is repetitively misused and perhaps overused. The written trace deteriorates as a direct result of a tense hand, leading to either outside criticism or self-criticism. Then either fear of more criticism or disgust at handwriting which may be perceived as ugly can lead to more tension and further pain.

3 Pain worsening at any time of extra tension in education, note taking, exams or later career as the demand for extra speed exacerbates the situation. As writing begins to fail, the writers ignore the warning of pain in their attempt to succeed in whatever task is required of them. The situation is aggravated by those with too high an expectation of the level required for any particular task: the perfectionists, the over-conventional or the socially insecure.

4 The pain and tension develop into involuntary movement or total inability to move the writing hand. This may develop through various stages of jerkiness. This can be observed in young people who appear to be on the way to writer's cramp. Tension may initially be noticed as excess pressure of the fingers on the pen or the pen on the paper, but it is the downward pressure of the whole hand on the desk that is more harmful. The pen then cannot move along the line, and the letters, such as they are, may be superimposed on each other. The elbow gets raised to release the pressure; replacing it produces a jerky movement. Keeping this movement up puts the strain on the upper arm, and that soon turns to more pain. Many cramp patients demonstrate their inability to write while resting their hand on the table, an echo of the time when it hurt to do so. The awkward and painful 'elbow raised' position is an unsuitable defensive strategy that has become automated.

This detailed explanation may help to an understanding of why some patients find that they can use a pen when the hand is completely unsupported on the writing surface, but then find it difficult to control either size of quality of writing. It also might explain why writer's cramp was less common a hundred years ago when people were carefully trained not to support the writing hand on the desk.

5   Physiological reasons can also contribute to this decline. Some patients have illustrated that atypical body proportions can mean that they were never able to be comfortable with standard furniture. In these circumstances, the resulting poor posture may well lead to pain when writing and contribute to the final condition. I have found, for example, some support for the idea that there is a correlation between long fingers and pain. It is not easy to displace overlong fingers on a pen – however fat the barrel.

As for the behavioural aspect, undoubtedly the writer's character plays a part. The more perfectionist writers may be in their nature, the more any deterioration in the standard of writing may worry them. This, in turn, starts the spiral of tension and pain which results in the writer focusing attention on the act of writing. Once the act of writing is no longer automated, it becomes slower and more stressful. More relaxed writers may take such matters in a more lighthearted and balanced way. Over-obedient people, who betray their character by still clinging closely to the model that they were taught in primary school, may be more prone to problems. This is because they are less likely to develop the personal shortcuts that enable them to speed up their handwriting. They may look upon such alterations, that are signs of maturity, as a deterioration in a self-imposed standard. Inventive people, purposely or subconsciously, may have already experimented to find quick personal solutions to simplifying letters and joins in order to create an efficient personal writing. These writers will be better equipped to deal with the increased demand for speed at key moments in their careers.

Commonsense explanations

It is possible to provide quite commonsense explanations for some of the aspects of writer's cramp that baffle the specialists who consider writer's cramp from an exclusively medical perspective. Statistically, it may be difficult to prove any of these points, even with the longitudinal study that is in preparation at present. Take just one point: the well-documented sequence of events that happens if the patient tries to overcome the cramp by changing the writing hand. The condition usually occurs in the second hand within five years.

This seems reasonable, looked at in a different way: if the patient changes writing hands without altering the attitudes that led to tension in the first place, then the cycle is likely to repeat itself. Patients who have been through such experiences tell me that when things start to go wrong with the second hand, the tension soon mounts. There is a rapid decline because of the worry that there is now no alternative, and they may soon have no means of writing.

There is an additional problem. When the natural hand is no longer capable of writing, some patients report that they seem to lose confidence in it. They explain how frightening is it when some part of their body ceases to obey their commands. The condition then seems to escalate: when the patients stop using their natural writing hand, it may eventually become unable to perform other movements, such as picking up a glass. Writing is more than a means of communication – it is oneself on paper. If you are successful, your writing reassures you; if it fails you, the constant visual reminder of your failure is there to torment you. Is this a possible explanation of how Sheehy and Marsden's dystonic stage of writer's cramp can commence?

Interfering with automatic movements

At some stage, this seemingly inexorable progress towards the serious condition of dystonia becomes a problem of the nervous system. Again, this may be able to be explained in fairly simple terms. When writers start to worry about their written trace, they focus their attention onto a movement that should be so well trained that it has long become internalised and automatic. This then interrupts the mechanism by which an automated action takes place and replaces it with a conscious effort. Once this happens, the tension involved in consciously producing and perfecting each stroke of written letters seems to make it increasingly difficult for the writer's hand to respond. This escalates as the writer strains even more to make his body react, reflecting this in an ever declining trace. Exactly the opposite is needed – the writer needs to forget all about the act of writing and let the motor memory deal with it.

There are plenty of precedents for this in everyday situations without referring to scientific papers. You can try out this idea of interrupting an automatic action with some complex trained movement that you are familiar with. What happens when you are driving your car and start wondering what your feet are doing on the pedals? What happens to your golf swing, tennis stroke or intricate dance routine when you start worrying about one small point in the chain of automatically trained movements of the muscles that are involved? Usually, the efficiency of whatever you have previously automated through lengthy motor training is disrupted Should you continue to be conscious of the details of what you are trying to perform, then tension will exacerbate the situation.

Dealing with the symptoms of writer's cramp

This involves three distinct phases:

1 New strategies for writing posture to fit in with individual needs – and a new penhold.
2 A new and realistic attitude to the concept of handwriting.
3 Help with the actual letterforms to show how personal short-cuts can save time, speed up writing and suit each writer's hand. It is also necessary to give writers a pride in their own trace and individuality.

The first point, about the importance of posture, table height, slanting writing surface, etc., is generally quite easy to explain and justify. All of this is detailed in Sassoon (1990) and other publications. Of all the aspects of posture, penhold is the most complex. Learning to assess the separate elements of hand and finger position as detailed in Sassoon, Wing and Nimmo-Smith (1986) is one matter. Deciding which alterations are likely to succeed with individuals is another. An initial success is of great importance when dealing with something that is so involved with a patient's self-confidence.

The other two parts of the treatment are unfamiliar to therapists of all medical disciplines. They are outside of their training and often even of their comprehension. This could be the reason why attempts at biofeedback, psychotherapy, hypnotism, etc., seldom succeed. Such treatments may help the patient in the important aspect of relaxing, but they do not deal in any depth in an informed way with the act of writing. Patients are not given the detailed practical help that equips them with less painful strategies for writing. This practical help is vital. With it comes self-confidence and motivation from the realisation that once again the production of a written trace is possible.

My technique is to question carefully against a background of knowledge gained from dealing with many cases of young people with problems, as well as with adult patients. It is important to discover the earliest possible cause of each patient's problem and to discuss how and when it started. If there is to be a hope that they can overcome the problem, patients must understand how the situation might have arisen. It is sometimes difficult to restore confidence in cases where patients have understood, or have actually been told by specialists, that their condition is incurable. I must assume that these techniques can alleviate the condition, or that in some cases it is reversible, and be able to pass this confidence on to my patients, otherwise it would be pointless to continue with my work.

Techniques for rehabilitation

Once the basic writing posture, table height and slant, paper position, etc., have been dealt with, the next step is to get patients to make some kind of mark with the hand that they are so sure they can never use again. There are many simple and almost devious ways of getting round this fear. If I am to be didactic, here is the place to be so. Never use the tripod grip at this stage, nor a conventional pen or pencil if you can avoid it. As far as the penhold is concerned, you should have no preconceived ideas about which unconventional penhold will first succeed. Remember that those without the usual complement of fingers manage to write well with most unconventional holds, and that the patient's conventional attitude to the act of writing is one of the concepts to be dealt with before he can understand and overcome this disability. A force grip is a good starter, but an unconventional writing implement will in itself usually bring a different hold. A spoon or stick to motion the letter in midair, a brush and paint, then a fat graphite block or charcoal is a suggested progression. When it comes to a more conventional implement, there should be a wide selection of modern pens for the patient to choose from. Patients are surprised to find how much an entirely different size or shape of pen-handle, or point, can alter the way their hand and their writing works.

Other quite simple techniques for the first session include motioning, then writing, with the eyes closed or with both hands simultaneously. These methods seem to work because the patient is no longer focusing on either the written trace or the problem hand, but depending on the internalised movement of the letter previously stored in the motor memory.

Once patients have written their name or even their initials, this is a comforting achievement. There is now something to work on and improve, thereby harnessing motivation and the basic human need to make a personal mark. Progress can be rapid; one session is sometimes enough even when a patient has been unable to write for several years. This may sound strange for therapists whose training will have prepared them to think in terms of a course of treatment. Once patients have been given new techniques and the confidence to go out and write again in a real-life situation, it is sometimes best to leave 'the cure' in their hands. It is important not to impose any preconceived ideas. Patients must be encouraged to experiment when they are relaxed and in their own homes. You can always be at the end of a phone if further encouragement is needed. In this way, patients can take the credit for their own recovery, because after the first stages it is really just a matter of returning confidence and the gradual relaxing of worry. Forgetting all about the way you write is what is needed, so constant reminders of a disability, particularly in a hospital environment, can be counterproductive.

A video is useful, not only for record keeping and future training sessions. Patients profit from seeing how quickly their movements have improved with new writing strategies. They are also helped by seeing how others in similar situations have progressed. Patients with dystonia seem to be isolated as well as frightened, and tend to think that they are unique. They are often ashamed of their involuntary movements, even when such movements may be almost undetectable to other people.

Conclusions

From the point of my own work, it is necessary to consider that:

1   Despite the fact that most of my patients have been referred by neurologists, I may have been dealing with patients where the original diagnoses might not have been quite accurate.
2   I have found that the very specific and localised complaint of writer's cramp is not always as serious or irreversible as has been previously thought – provided it is dealt with in an informed way.
3   Perhaps the symptoms have different causes or several triggers.

Whichever of these conclusions is most valid in any particular case, the argument must be that, for the sake of patients, the medical profession should begin to reconsider its approach to writer's cramp. Attitudes need to be altered about handwriting and with them the image of what is a taught, and not a natural, skill. There needs to be a widening of focus to reconsider the distinction between what is termed 'normal' and what is 'abnormal' – and to determine whether in some cases it is not necessary to consider writer's cramp as a medical problem at all. Cases where unnecessarily narrow conventional attitudes have been contributory factors in the onset of the condition of writer's cramp illustrate this point. These conclusions are a plea for cooperation, and not for confrontation, with the medical profession.

Handwriting samples of the patient over twenty years

Specific Latent Heat of Fusion
   The specific latent heat of fusi
is defined as the quantity of he

Teenaged at school

Total energy of electron in box = $-W + \frac{1}{2} mv^2$
a first approximation, the electron box may b

At university showing decreased size and a tremor

l the maxcium for coxple solo
butarostamrole, bromorphenyl dehyde

Palm Research limited was established
Palmer Research limited a. estab'

During the consultation

Consolidation as market leader in Brew=
Bam has rationalised its production
system to be a low cost producer
nationwide outlet and natural

After four more years (by then in the mid-thirties).

CHAPTER 7

Writer's Cramp: A Case Study

This paper was presented at the Fifth Conference of the International Graphonomics Society, in Arizona in 1991. It was not considered for publication in the volume of papers from that conference because it was about to be published in this book. In the case of this particular paper I regret the decision. I would have liked this work to have the widest possible exposure. Writer's cramp patients deserve their condition to be understood. This case study had been specially chosen because it was one of a very few where it had been possible to monitor the patient's progress over a period of several years. I feel it important to reproduce this paper in full here even though the first paragraph may seem to repeat some of the material from the previous chapter.

A movement disorder or just a handwriting problem?

Writer's cramp has long been considered a neurological condition, a form of dystonia, and is often thought to be incurable. Recent publications such as Sheehy and Marsden (1982), which reviews recent research as well as defining certain details of writer's cramp, and Hughes and McLellan (1985) further our knowledge of the neurological perspective of the condition. Hughes and McLellan suggest; '. . . that writing is prone to dystonia because of the two concurrent requirements. The first is to hold the pen securely in the fingers and keep it applied evenly to the paper. The second is to permit rapid and very fine modulation of activity in the co-activating muscles.' Neither papers give suggestions, however, for therapeutic techniques that might help patients to regain their ability to write.

This paper builds on the overview of five years' research in the field of remediating writer's cramp, reported in the previous chapter. It introduces a well-documented case that supports the theories put forward in that paper: that writer's cramp can be the result of a combination of relatively minor factors built up over a period of years, culminating in tension, pain and finally an inability to perform the act of writing.

The case reported here, of a man in his early thirties, was chosen for several reasons. Handwriting samples were available dating back to the patient's school days. In addition his medical records were available. His symptoms combined most of those documented as common to a sample of patients treated over a period of five years as reported in the previous chapter, but his remediation consisted of only one session. Follow-up over a period of four years has been by post, with an annual handwriting sample and progress report

This patient had been diagnosed by three separate neurologists on three separate occasions over a period of over ten years as suffering from writer's cramp. The case shows, however, that a detailed explanation can lead a patient to an understanding of what factors may have led to his condition. Furthermore, this understanding may be all that is necessary to enable some patients to self-correct, regain confidence and resume writing. The basis of the understanding is that whatever personal differences between patients, the problem that needs addressing is each individual's handwriting strategy, posture and attitude to the act of writing.

Case history

This patient was a high-achieving, trouble-free pupil during his school years, winning prizes for handwriting. His problems arose during his second year at university. He reported: 'I began to notice that some letters were not being formed as I thought they should, such as the 'a', where the upper horizontal part would not join with the vertical stem. If I tried to decrease the speed of writing, the letters still would not form properly. This aberration seemed to become gradually more acute until I found it difficult to draw the chemical symbols'. However, the patient passed an important written examination at the end of his second year. The third and final year became progressively stressful. The patient reported: 'I was unable to take adequate notes and I distinctly remember that the pen seemed to be forced out of my hand because whenever I held a pen the fourth and fifth fingers tried to straighten so that I could not grip the pen as I had been accustomed.' He experimented with various types of writing implements but reports: 'Remembering all the adverse comments about ball-points at school, I tried to conduct all writing with a fountain pen.'

In the Easter vacation he became worried about revising and writing his final papers. He then consulted his general practitioner who, after diagnosing writer's cramp, referred him to a neurologist at his local hospital. This specialist suggested that he should learn to write with his left hand. This idea was rejected by the patient who realised that he would be unable to become sufficiently practised in the eight weeks available. Returning to his university he was seen by a professor of neurology who repeated the diagnosis of writer's cramp and arranged for him to have an amanuensis. This enabled him to pass his final chemistry examinations, but with a lower grade than expected. The patient explained how difficult it was to adapt to using such a procedure. As he put it, 'I had no experience in instructing him in setting out answers on my behalf.'

During the following ten years he did not take up the suggestion of using his left hand but instead he avoided the task of writing whenever possible. As he described the situation, 'Although less acute than when at college, the unsteadiness and restricted movement has remained and this has limited my ability in note-taking at meetings.' He noted that he felt this was associated with adrenalin levels so, 'In the mornings or when in any kind of stressful situation, even so minor as unfamiliar surroundings, my writing (at the time of consultation in 1987) is still unsteady, shaky and poorly formed.'

He consulted a leading neurologist when his career dictated the need for further professional training. As he put it, he did not want to go through the same ordeal again that he had as an undergraduate. A diagnosis of writer's cramp was again given, followed by referral to a therapist. An occupational therapist gave him what he described as 'manual dexterity tests'. Relaxation techniques were suggested, but no practical guidance for the resumption of writing was given. This persistent patient did not give up but spent many hours practising exercises in an attempt to regain the 'Marion Richardson' style that had served him so well at school. When that failed he set about finding, as he put it, 'an expert in the mechanics of handwriting'.

Some contributory factors observed during the session
1 His height (6' 3"), hand size and the length of his fingers
2 His evident tension about the long-standing condition and the resulting inability to write that was holding back his career
3 His perfectionist approach to letterforms, and his conventional attitudes to writing posture

The following steps were amongst those taken to help the patient to understand how his condition had arisen

1 All attempts to help make him comfortable at a table were unsuccessful. His height and long arms together made it difficult to find a suitable paper position. It was suggested that he should rest the paper, at an angle on his lap. In this way he understood that his height had probably contributed to his discomfort, and eventual pain, when writing. It is interesting to note that his observation on being told that it might be a

good idea to write on his lap was, 'Am I allowed to?' This comment from an Oxford graduate shows how much a conventional view of the act of writing can override common-sense attitudes to the relief of discomfort while writing.

2   The length of his fingers was likely to have increased this discomfort. A survey of the incidence of pain undertaken with a sample of 100 teenage writers, reported in Sassoon (1990), had already indicated a correlation between pain and long fingers. This survey had used a diagnostic questionnaire drawn up by a neurologist with an interest in writer's cramp. Alternative penholds were suggested as a way of relaxing his hand but they were rejected by him in the first instance as too unconventional for his perception of the act of writing.

3   The patient had high expectations of presentation and letterforms, still referring to his prize-winning efforts at school at the age of ten. It was explained to him that perfect letterforms could not be attained at speed. It was arched letters such as 'n' that were most painful for him to write and he considered that they were the ones most affected by tremor. It was therefore demonstrated to him how most adults modify these letters at speed, and that adult handwriting should not be expected to retain the perfection of a juvenile taught model.

4   It was explained to him that as no specialist had been able to indicate any other neurological condition, and that ten years had passed since the original diagnosis, the alterations in handwriting strategy, posture and attitudes might lead to a solution of his problems. In that case no further treatment would be needed. The returning confidence in a patient's ability to write without pain, plus the decreasing physical and mental tension should lead to the re-automating of the act of writing. Once the conscious emphasis on the act recedes, the remaining tension should further decrease.

5   It was requested that he should go home and write up his own case with the understanding that he had now gained of some of the possible causes.

As a scientist himself, the logical explanation and positive approach appealed to the patient. Telephone contact was kept up in the early months, as it was necessary to allay worries about a slight residual tremor. As this disappeared after a few months, it may be assumed

The patient had unusually long fingers and it seemed a wise precaution to ask for a print of his hand. It has not been possible, despite many discussions with those whose knowledge of the physiology of the hand far exceeds my own, to ascertain what particular points to measure in order to make comparisons with other, perhaps more 'average' hands.

Hand print reduced to 75% of the original size.

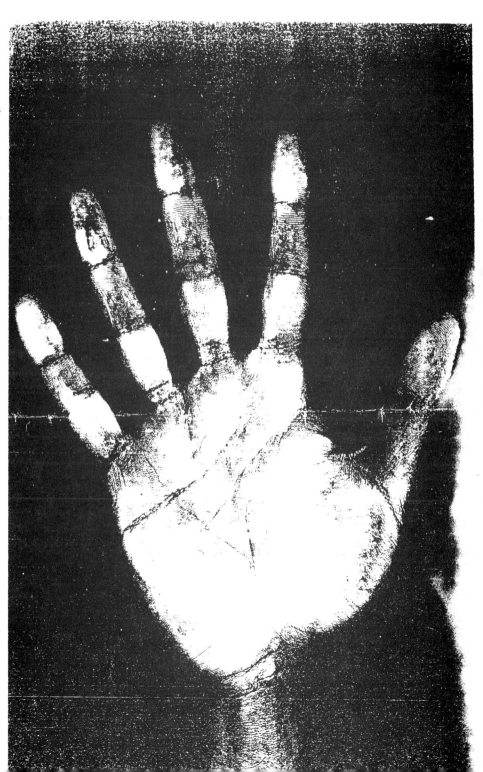

to have been a tension tremor. Thereafter an annual letter marked his handwriting and career progress, the first one reporting on his post-graduate examination success.

No further writing problems occurred in this case, which has followed the pattern of several others in the past four years. It must, however, be borne in mind that there is no assurance that a similar dystonia may not be an early indicator of some neurological or other condition. Should this be the future for a proportion of patients, then at least their ability to write may have been extended. The purpose of this presentation is not to claim a cure, but to demonstrate that with a specialist knowledge of handwriting problems, cases of writer's cramp that are often considered incurable may be amenable to remediation.

Discussion

This patient's detailed report gives us many clues to the causes of his complaint and provides pointers for the rehabilitation of others. Some of his remarks, as well as those of other patients, some of which are reported in Sassoon (Spring 1990), give an insight into the frustrations that exacerbate their condition. The statements reproduced below come from his original report in 1987 and a further letter written retrospectively in 1991. As well as giving a patient's views concerning his condition and his treatment, they give certain clues to his personality.

'I did not believe that there was anything wrong neurologically as I could perform other manual tasks such as playing the piano.'

'Medical advice initially ranged from disbelief to unhelpful. I particularly objected to my GP's reaction that I was inventing a problem as a means of avoiding examinations. I believe the associated stress and frustration may well aggravate the writing difficulties. Hence it really is essential to obtain advice at an early stage.' In relation to the occupational therapist: 'He provided me with a plastic pen grip but I did not have any confidence in the advice and observations proffered by this man.'

'I reckoned that the stress that I felt at certain times was aggravated by my lacking confidence in being able to write and also being dissatisfied with the artistic aspects of the output.'

It is interesting to note that in none of his written reports did the patient record the two key issues that he discussed at length during the consultation and afterwards on the telephone: pain, and the fear that despite his own commonsense attitude, he had a grave neurological condition

Pain in this case was not confined to the hand. It extended up his arm and to his neck. As with most writer's cramp patients, pain seems to be one of the main factors that lead to this condition. It is unusual that he should not think it worth recording, but this omission ties in with surveys of teenagers. A proportion of those who experience pain seem to have an expectation that the act of handwriting should be painful, so have not thought it worth reporting to either parents or teachers until specifically questioned.

This patient discussed at length his worries about the possibility of suffering from some additional undiagnosed neurological condition. He continued over the first few weeks to worry that the slight residual tremor was a serious indication and his access to medical journals only caused him further stress. In other cases where the term 'incurable dystonia' had been used and patients directed to the Dystonia Society, even further unnecessary anxiety had been caused.

Four years on the patient reports: 'I am certainly no longer worried that handwriting will limit my ability to perform to maximum effect when required. Note taking can sometimes be difficult in meetings where I feel tense, but then I note a few comments at the time and write a full summary on the PC after the meeting. Looking back, I believe the writer's cramp problem was a symptom of stress – a fear of slow or illegible handwriting adversely affecting examination results – at school, university and in professional life.' This statement highlights the need for a therapist to be realistic. Such patients must be reminded that although their symptoms can be alleviated it may not be possible to eliminate the causes of stress entirely, and that a handwriting will always mirror the attitude and condition of the writer at any particular moment. At moments of great stress some of the symptoms may reappear but, with understanding, this need not cause real anxiety. A perfectionist attitude also appears to be part of the profile of writer's cramp patients, and this characteristic is not easily overcome either.

The patient continues: 'If the problems that I experienced with handwriting are not rare, the subject should have a sufficiently high profile that GPs and educational establishments will recognise the problem and have some form of counselling available.'

A few comments must be added. Stress management alone is useless. In addition to counselling, informed advice on dealing with handwriting strategies and attitudes as outlined in *Handwriting: A New Perspective,* Sassoon (1990) is needed. Increasing numbers of patients are being referred with writer's cramp worldwide. The incidence in younger pupils in countries where the educational systems are particularly competitive is worrying. Computers cannot perform all the tasks that we do by hand. Until a realistic and flexible attitude to the level of handwriting expected under pressure of speed is widespread, those perfectionists with a high aesthetic expectation will be at risk. Any occurrence of pain when writing should be taken seriously, and the writer at any age should be counselled to experiment to find more comfortable strategies. Until more people understand the relationship between modern pens and alternative penholds, many more will suffer discomfort rather than experiment with something that they might think 'odd' or unconventional, or that they might think other people would mock. Writing posture and paper position also contribute to either painful or pain-free writing. This all adds up to informed consideration for the writer as well as the reader. Worldwide a method of teaching handwriting is needed that works on the principle of encouraging not only neat handwriting but fast handwriting. Models that lead to efficient personal handwriting need to be taught, so that high achievers can acquire a hand that records their thoughts and takes their notes at sufficient speed.

Cases with more serious symptoms than those of the patient recorded in this paper, some with considerable involuntary movement or where the disability had spread to affect other hand skills, and occasionally to other limbs, have responded to similar treatment. The patients' comments have also been recorded. They describe, for instance, how it feels when the hand no longer obeys the dictate of the mind.

While not wishing to confront neurologists, psychiatrists and occasionally surgeons who make their diagnoses according to their specialties, it must be in the interests of patients to report on this work. As reported in the previous chapter, greater success has been experienced when, in a minority of cases, such as this one, patients have not been seen in a hospital environment. It is far easier then to give them a handwriting perspective rather than a medical one. In a neurologist's own department it is not easy to persuade patients that their best chance of writing again is to assume that there is little wrong with them. To question a specialist's diagnosis in front of therapists who are there to observe and learn these techniques is far from diplomatic. Whereas most patients are just relieved to have found a solution to their problems, the occasional one, not without good reason, has considered a formal complaint if not legal proceedings. When it is realised that in some cases patients have given up well-paid jobs after a prognosis of incurable dystonia, this may be understandable. Solly wrote in 1864, 'Upon your correct diagnosis may depend the health and happiness of your patient. If you mistake its real nature and regard it as incipient sign of the softening of the brain – a mistake that I have known to occur – you may destroy the happiness of your patient and bring on the very disease which you have erroneously diagnosed.' This train of thought could be extended to say that when neurologists proclaim that writer's cramp is an incurable neurological complaint, then that is what is sometimes induced. When a psychiatrist (as an eminent one did to another patient of mine) insists that writer's cramp is a phobia and prescribes holding a pen for an hour a day as a cure for pain, then a phobia is what he is likely to induce.

It is not easy to subject the techniques, explained in more detail in the previous chapter, to scientific scrutiny, as would be customary in many other circumstances. A longitudinal study had been proposed by the hospital that provided the majority of my patients. A proposal was put forward but has fallen through owing to lack of funds or maybe just lack of interest. My own view is that to request an annual report of patients' progress, in their own words and from the relaxed atmosphere of their own home, is a fair way of assessing their return to writing. Carrying out regular tests in a hospital environment might, in my opinion, adversely affect the patients' chances of regaining a relaxed handwriting by constantly reminding them of their worries about a serious neurological condition. Such tension would inhibit the writer, be reflected in any handwriting sample and to a certain extent invalidate any findings.

Part 2

builds on the findings of my research, and presents an overview of my work in schools and hospitals. The insights gained through such experience are reported. It is shown how they were used to advise curriculum planners worldwide, and as a basis for educational and medical lecturing - with all the advantages of discussion with informed audiences.

The book ends where it began, with letterforms and calligraphy, but looking at these subjects from unusual angles, first the teaching of letterforms to children for educational and therapeutic purposes, and finally an analytical look at my original craft from a psychological perspective.

CHAPTER 8

How Much Do We Know about Handwriting?

Introduction

The second part of this book consists of excerpts from articles and reports that together illustrate how information gained from my research was disseminated. They are not necessarily reproduced in chronological order although in many cases their commissioning played a part in the direction that my work proceeded. My editorial for a special handwriting edition of the journal *Visible Language* forms the basis of this introduction, focusing as much on what we do not know about the subject as what it is claimed that we do. It starts by asking whether we are asking the right questions to provide valid answers to many of the pressing problems that need to be solved in education today and continues to looks more deeply into some of the issues. One persistent difficulty that needs addressing is the frequent inability of one discipline, within the many involved in handwriting studies, to comprehend another's terms. We must ask whether there is a precise enough terminology for letters, not only to communicate with each other, but to inform and detail individual investigations.

It is the underlying need to consider the many facets of the act of writing that actually limits the relevance of so much handwriting research. Unless the researchers who design a project have some understanding of the complex nature of handwriting before they start, then their conclusions, if not their detailed findings, may be limited or, worse still, distorted by too narrow a view.

Attitudes to handwriting

The personal quality of handwriting needs special consideration at all levels of research. It is not only the effects of such individuality but the inevitability and desirability of personal differences that need to be stressed. Once it is accepted that handwriting is a reflection of the writer on paper, then the perspective shifts – in research, in diagnosis and in educational planning. The perception of writers through their writing may still be an unfamiliar one to therapists or doctors whether they are assessing neurological impairment, for example, psychiatric disorder or even senility. It requires considerable application to analyse and interpret the written trace, and at the same time the writers' perception of themselves should not be forgotten. Whether it is ill-health, immaturity, frenzy or perhaps just laziness that is mirrored in a personal handwriting, certain messages would be evident both to the reader and to the writer. Some of these indications may be more distressful to the writer than to anyone else, causing them to seek remedial help. Where the writing problem is a reflection of the writer's condition it cannot be 'cured' by cosmetic techniques such as trying to copy a new model. The root cause needs to be diagnosed and explained before there is a hope of any real improvement.

When the same attitudes are related to education, a whole range of other issues are raised. Teachers' (and parents') perception of children through their writing cannot be ignored. Judgements and criticisms are made that can harm pupils' self-confidence and with it their ability to relax and progress in a satisfactory way with their written work. Where many of these judgements are coloured only by a measurement of 'neatness' or by how well children may be following an arbitrarily imposed school model, even more problems are likely to arise. Handwriting models rouse strong emotions. There is a proliferation of proponents for a wide variety of different letterforms, all aimed at being the ideal solution to handwriting problems. The need for a model in the early stages is not questioned. The questions that really need addressing are: first, how soon a model should be dropped to enable the writer to develop a consistent personal hand; and second, what are the long-term effects of imposing certain (or any) models longer than absolutely necessary?

When it comes to handwriting there is another issue that is often ignored: the writer deserves as much consideration as the reader. Standardisation in handwriting may, in certain circumstances, suit the reader, but the pressure for identical letterforms can only disadvantage the majority of writers. It is accepted that handwriting is for communicating and therefore it must be legible. If teachers, however, were to analyse what is illegible, rather than the other way round, they might come nearer to an understanding of the subject. The few points that make handwriting unreadable do indeed need dealing with, but these are seldom aesthetic points. They are more often concerned with the movement, height differentials and spacing of basic letters.

Educating educators about handwriting

The narrowness of much educational research continues to contribute to the school policies that allow handwriting problems to arise. What actually happens in our schools? Details of how handwriting is taught or of groups or individuals' specific performance come very high on the list of subjects that we know little about. Sassoon (1988) looked at the effects of different models and methods on how children learn to write, but had first to evolve simple ways of analysing handwritten letters that might inform those whose training did not include a specialist knowledge of letterforms.

The same body of work included a critical review of recent educational research. It revealed work that used inappropriate tasks and inadequate samples to provide norms of various aspects of handwriting. It revealed examples that had been copied by adults to resemble schoolchildrens' work in papers that have considerable influence on educational policies. It also revealed an unfortunate tendency for some of these questionable papers to be repeatedly quoted while others with less sensational or expedient findings, based on more thorough research, were consistently ignored. Perhaps the most worrying finding in this review was how frequently researchers depended on subjective judgements of legibility to justify their hypothesis or preferred model. When more closely investigated, many of these judgements appeared to be made more on aesthetic criteria or on fashionable details than on actual factors that are likely to affect legibility.

All these somewhat emotive points need to be seen in perspective and are discussed at length in the thesis quoted above, for those who want further details. With these points in mind, however, this might be a good time and place to give a few pointers for those whose work requires that they depend on the findings of handwriting research for educational planning.

Some questions for the readers of research papers to ask themselves

1 Does the task that the pupils were given bear any resemblance to the tasks that you expect to be undertaken in the circumstances in which you work? In a classroom situation 'writing' combines various cognitive functions – spelling, grammar and creativity – with the act of handwriting. So, for example, a task consisting of a phrase repeated over a period of time to yield a so-called norm may be misleading. A task that involves a lot of copying may measure writers' copying capacity, not their motor skills; likewise results from a dictated task may be influenced by the hesitancy or fluency in varying spelling capacities.

2 How specific are the criteria and are they relevant to you? Was it undertaken in your country or elsewhere? If so, was the educational policy similar to your own? Do the pupils start school at the same age? Wherever the study took place, did the attitude to models and methods resemble that used in your school/district/country?

3 Does the study consider only the written trace or does it also look at how the trace was produced – taking into account such matters as penhold and paper position?

4 Does it consider the degree of training involved? Conclusions can be misleading if drawn from situations where either little training has been given so poor strategies are evident, or alternatively, particularly thorough training has been given. When information has been gathered from questionnaires, there is a further point to consider. Where only a stated proportion of questionnaires has been returned, readers should ask themselves whether the findings from such work reflect only the most concerned teachers rather than a representative sample of those approached.

5 Does any work that tries to justify the use of a particular model or method look at the long-term affects of such teaching? If the

study, for whatever reason, cannot be longitudinal it should attempt to show how pupils with similar training have managed later on their school life, in particular how they have managed to personalise their letterforms to deal with stress and the increased demands for speed.

6 By what means is the final product assessed? In particular, it is advisable to be wary of legibility assessments that tend to be subjective, however impressive their test and retest results may appear. Legibility is likely to be in the mind of the reader and dependent on many factors, such as expectation, familiarity, personal training and tastes.

Unfortunately, handwriting is often taken for granted, and its complexity as a task ignored by many of those who profess to be experts in one aspect or another. Modern technology enables us to investigate some areas of handwriting in great detail while leaving other equally important ones unexplained. Something that many of us still depend on every day of our lives is perhaps less understood today than it was several hundred, or maybe even several thousand years ago.

This illustrates how the use of a slanting writing surface and the alternative penhold helped a child with cerebral palsy to control her tremor. Both these illustrations are reproduced from Sassoon (1991) Handwriting: The Way to Teach it.

I would like this page to have two functions. The first is to be a tribute to my great friend Pat Savage who, by her accurate and beautiful drawings from my hasty classroom photographs, has illuminated my books over the years. As well as the drawings on this page, the hands that appear in several different chapters of this book are her work. The second purpose of this page is to draw attention once again to the importance of writing posture when planning a curriculum or in everyday classroom situations.

This drawing illustrates the interaction between paper position and body posture. This awkward situation arose because of a slight error in an otherwise excellent curriculum document. Right-handers were taught to place their paper centrally instead of to the side of their writing hand. They were then instructed to twist it and many of them followed those instructions only too well.

CHAPTER 9

Education and Curriculum Planning

Lessons from the past

This part of the book brings together a variety of articles and reports concerned with educational planning around the world. However I would like to begin with a backward glance. It was not until I was asked to plan an up-to-date handwriting policy for the London Montessori Centre that I looked in detail at what this great educationist wrote about the subject during the first half of the twentieth century. Maria Montessori had an enlightened way of looking at handwriting that has not been surpassed in the intervening years, and those who write about handwriting today would do well to study her work. Her attitude to letterforms is as relevant today as when she wrote: 'Even though we use the same alphabet the motions we make are so individual that each one of us has his own particular style of writing, and there are as many forms of writing as there are of man.' This reminds us that the way individuals use their bodies, and their differing hand movements in particular, affect the letters that they produce. Many years before the idea that handwriting is a motor skill was generally discussed, Montessori was referring to the 'muscle memory'. She explained that the purpose of early handwriting exercises is to stock the 'muscle memory'.

Montessori showed how little has altered when she described how all too often 'Writing is the result of painful and disagreeable preparation in school. It evokes the memory of dry effort, of pains suffered and disagreeable preparation in school.' She wrote with some emotion of the explosion into writing that four-year-old children experienced under her guidance and left us with useful guidance as to when children might be able to start to write. She explained how children between the age of four and five enjoyed the pre-writing exercises exemplified by the touching of her famous sandpaper letters with their eyes closed. She warned, 'If on the other hand the exercise is given to a child who is too old, to one, for example, who is six years old, he will be more interested in seeing the letter which represents a sound and is used in words, and the attraction of the touch will not be sufficient to interest him in the exercises of movement.

I cannot say that Montessori influenced my own ideas about handwriting. These came about as a result of my own observations and research. It was not until much later that I read her work in detail. The point is that the truths about handwriting are not new. They were known and written about by the writing masters of the fifteenth century, although in terms appropriate to the tools and usage of that day, as much as they were in Montessori's day, or Marion Richardson's.

Observing handwriting in other countries

To understand what is happening to handwriting today it is necessary to look in some detail into what happens in other countries, where educational policies and maybe other cultural factors affect the teaching of handwriting. Whenever I have been fortunate enough to have been asked to visit a country to advise on some aspect of a national handwriting policy, I have come away feeling that I have learned and profitted more than the host country. Sometimes I have had to write reports for boards or departments of education, but it seems a breach of confidence to quote directly from them, so I am confining this section to a few isolated observations.

Occasionally such a visit has provided an opportunity to observe some aspect of writing that previously I have only considered theoretically. Take left-handedness: one European country, when asked what policy they had for left-handers, replied that they did not have any left-handed children. There appeared to be no more indications of trouble in the schools than we have with 15% of our children using the left hand to write. Another country had such a good policy for dealing with left-handers' handwriting that in every school that I visited I was told that the left-handers were the high achievers and far more problems were encountered with right-handers. In mainland China I accepted what I was told – that it was better for children to use their right hand because of the left-to-right sequencing of Chinese characters. In Chinese schools away from the mainland, however, I saw several left-handers managing the correct sequencing quite easily, and only one child who needed to be guided to change hands because of severe directional problems.

It may be that visitors are taken to carefully selected schools, but in one district in a Scandinavian country I saw whole schools where the level of writing was so high that pupils seemed unable to relax their calligraphic standard and speed up enough to use handwriting naturally. Even at the age of 16, pupils still wrote carefully in pencil on alternate sets of four staved lines. The level of pain seemed to me quite unacceptable, as it was in a certain expensive Australian school where 28 out of 29 boys, and their teacher, reported pain when writing. There the walls were covered with calligraphic patterns that would have done credit to a professional scribe, but the teacher said 'Of course hand writing hurts, it is a discipline.'

I have been to places where beautifully designed adjustable furniture was available, looking ideal in an empty classroom, but where in use, all the chairs and tables were still at the minimum height. When asked why they were not better used, and the children were still inappropriately seated, the teacher's answer seemed at first to be somewhat destructive. He explained that it was too disruptive to be always altering the heights. This alerted me, however, to the very real problems of adjustable furniture when pupils are constantly changing classrooms. It made me more appreciative of a more formal arrangement in a different country, where there were three sets of chairs and tables, ranked in lines, the largest at the back, for pupils to be seated according to size.

There are times when I have had to focus on issues that are relevant to the situation in one particular country at a particular moment. In 1990 the education authorities in Western Australia had to abandon a project that I had been working on with them over a few years. We had hoped to introduce a flexible handwriting scheme that was more concerned with method than the imposition of any particular model. It would have needed intensive in-service training and suddenly there was not enough money to proceed. Instead, at rather short notice, it was decided to adopt the model currently in use in several other Australian states. This was quite satisfactory, except for the fact that there still was little allowance for the depth of in-service training needed to make the change. The following article was written in an attempt to retain some of the flexibility of the scheme that we had hoped to introduce. I understand that a shortened version was sent to every school in the state, but its relevance is not confined to any particular country or period of time.

ISSUES TO DEAL WITH WHEN CHANGING TO A NEW HANDWRITING MODEL

From time to time individual schools, districts, states or even whole countries may decide to alter their handwriting model. Any such change should be preceded by considerable research, particularly into the effects that the teaching of that particular model is likely to have on secondary schoolchildren's performance. Such research is seldom carried out, and it has yet to be proven that any particular model is significantly more successful in the long run than any other.

This paper was written in 1991 for the Curriculum Development Branch of the Ministry of Education of Western Australia. It was at a time that they had been directed to introduce an unfamiliar model into all their schools.

Whatever the reason for changing – even if it is only following the latest fashion – it is usually in the hope that the new model will improve children's handwriting performance. If such improvement is to take place then it is important to understand the underlying implications. Briefly these are:

1 A model in itself does not teach handwriting. The method is more important than any model, and the teacher who teaches is most important of all.
2 It may be difficult for teachers and children alike to become accustomed to a new model.
3 No model is going to suit everyone, and there will be some for whom the change will present real problems. It will then have to be decided whether such children, and those who already have a satisfactory handwriting, will have to alter for the sake of uniformity.

This brings up the basis on which a model is used. It should be as a guide for the early stages, a help to both teachers and pupils, but not as an inflexible tool. The purpose of teaching handwriting must always be borne in mind: it is to provide the writer with a legible, fast means of communication, flexible enough to deal with the variety of tasks needed in school and later life. Everyday handwriting need not be calligraphy, and the training need not be the exact copying of letters more suited to a life as a forger.

Understanding the alterations in letterforms

To many people, altering the model might seem to be only a matter of changing to a different shape of letters, more pleasing to the eye, or perhaps with a more modern look. It is not so simple for the writer. Writing is a motor skill, and those letters on the page are a result of a movement of the hand and arm. Children are trained in a certain movement to produce a certain type of letter. If they have to alter the model then they have to learn a new movement. Certain models require specific manipulation of the pen and therefore the hand, to produce certain details such as entry strokes, exits, slant or even complete idiosyncratic letters. Children and teachers alike will have to unlearn the familiar movement for a particular letter, that will have long been stored in their motor memory and produced automatically when writing at speed. A new movement will have to be learned and be as habitual as the old one before fluent 'automatic' writing can be resumed. This matter of automatic writing is important. Writers should not have to be thinking about the form of the letters that they write, as they proceed along the line. The stress of having to conform to an exact model, whether familiar or not, may impinge on their ability to write fast and consistently.

This relationship between the movement of the hand and the written trace must be considered at all times. This should colour the way teachers approach the teaching of any model. If certain children are not managing to conform to the model it may well be that the way they are sitting, placing their paper or holding the pen may be inhibiting the production of the specific slant or proportion of the letters they are supposed to be copying. Then certain decisions will have to be taken. The proportion and slant of letters are likely to be the result of manipulation of the fingers and rotation of the wrist and therefore to a certain extent beyond the control of a young child. We all use our bodies in slightly different ways, our own proportions are different, so there can be no exact rules on matters affecting writing posture. The subtle differences are mirrored in our writing therefore to be too strict about the pursuit of any model is likely to be counterproductive in real terms.

Dealing with real problems arising from a model

One of the easiest ways of considering the problems involved is to see a new model through the eyes of a left-hander. Some left-handers are likely to have some difficulty in producing a forward slant. They may also have considerable problems with the angle of entry and exit strokes. Are they going to be constantly chastised for something that they can do little about, at the same time developing a distaste for the act of writing and curtailing their creative writing efforts as they struggle to copy a form or detail of letters that is particularly difficult for them? Dyspraxic children may have conquered an approximation of the old model after a lot of effort, but might face considerable problems with a new one. It seems that the model should always be seen in perspective. Where it is helpful to enforce it, where the children are happy and consistent in the elements of any particular model, then all is well. However teachers should always be on the lookout for those for whom the model is not working well, and those for whom it is positively harmful. Sadly this will occur amongst a proportion of children with any model in almost any classroom. It should not be seen as a sign of weakness then to encourage individuality, and to help such children to develop the slight personal differences that will make consistent writing easier for them. This is a child-orientated attitude but certainly is not the easy option for teachers, because it means that they will need a wider knowledge of letters and how they work.

Perceiving the differences

Letterforms are a special study and quite outside most people's field, so it is not surprising that when it comes to a new model it is not easy for teachers, parents or children to analyse the differences between it and the old one. Leaving children aside, adults may have considerable problems perceiving and producing certain details of letters if they do not resemble their own personal handwriting.

Your own style is part of what you were taught and part of what you are as a person. It becomes so automatic that when you try to relate to letters that are unfamiliar you may disregard some details and exaggerate others. Even something as measurable as slant can be incorrectly reproduced if it is different to the writer's own hand. When it comes to details such as entry and exit strokes then

An Australian model with curved entry strokes to 'm' 'n' and 'r' and a midline exit to the letter 'o'.

m n

o p q r

The word 'on' shows how confusing this combination is. When the teacher misinterprets the entry to the letter 'r' in the word 'or', it is even more ridiculous.

on

or

the real problems arise. These two elements of letters vary from model to model, sometimes arbitrarily but sometimes with real purpose, so it is worth understanding more about them. The exit strokes are the important ones. Exit strokes on letters that terminate on the baseline train the hand in the onward movement that is helpful in the development of a flowing joined writing.

With the old print scripts the letters and the hand stopped abruptly at the baseline. The hand became used to exerting maximum pressure there to ensure neatness. This is exactly the opposite to the movement required for joining, when the hand needs to alter direction and lessen the pressure simultaneously. With a new model it is important to notice and try to replicate the angle of the baseline exits, because these strokes have two functions. They train in the onward movement as explained, but they also affect the spacing between letters. An acute exit leads to close spacing and a flatter angle of exit leads to wider spacing. Exit strokes on letters that end on the mid-line such as 'o','w' or 'v' can be confusing. If they are learned as an integral part of the letter they can cause problems at the joining stage as they may be at the wrong angle in some combinations of letters. Designers of models need to think clearly about these points and to understand the implications on more mature forms of letters. Teachers who are faced with details of prescribed models that prove difficult to work with should be allowed to adapt them for the benefit of their pupils.

This would apply to entry strokes even more so. They are neither essential nor always desirable, although they are retained in certain models for a variety of reasons. These reasons range from a desire to promote the over-curve movement to a rather mistaken idea that they show where an exit stroke ends and the next letter begins. The problem with entry strokes is that they are dependent on the height of the preceding exit and like 'top' exits, they are likely to cause problems at the joining stage. In addition there are two distinct angles of entries: one that comes up into the top of a downstroke, and another that rolls into and over the top of it. If you use one in your personal writing it is very difficult to be consistent in reproducing it in another classroom model. If the wrong angle of entry is taught with a new model then it is going to distort the letters, because those entries are specific to certain proportions of letters and sit oddly on any others.

Education involves parents as well as teachers and children. Parents and even grandparents may influence the way children perceive handwriting. Children may also be influenced by their friend's style or that of other adults whom they admire. An abrupt break from a traditional model may not only encounter parental opposition, but children may also find it disruptive from a stylistic preference. Such situations need careful defusing otherwise they can provoke considerable antagonism and unnecessary frustration.

Once again it is a good idea to be flexible and understanding. Such feelings may be deep-rooted, and considerable unhappiness could be caused by forcing such children to change. If these children are tactfully dealt with they may end up wanting to alter if they can see positive advantages as their peers learn a new model. If not, then it is likely that such strongly felt preferences will provide any particular pupils with a mature hand most suited to their personality.

When to drop a model

The time to adopt a model presents an easy decision – it must be from the start. The time to drop a model in the best interests of children is far harder. This brings us back to the real purpose of a model. The most important aspects of learning to write are independent of the model. The rules that govern our writing system, the direction of writing, the movement of the basic letters and the height differentials that are essential to later legibility, as well as the spacing between letters and between words They are common to all models, and far more important than any specific shape, slant or proportion of letters. However, both teacher and children may need a model to start with but once it has done its job any model that is too strictly enforced can start to work against children's best interest. This is why handwriting must be seen against the wider perspective of the pupil's whole school life and not confined to the ease of teaching in the first few years. Once basic separate letters are working well, and then basic joins, it is time to let children experiment to find the personal variations in letterforms. These variations, along with the subtle shortcuts between letters, make up an efficient writing that will speed up and become consistent for each individual. If handwriting exercises are continued, with constant reference to a model, past the stage that is essential, this experimentation is inhibited. This was a real problem with the old continuous cursives. Children were so drilled in a continuous movement that there was no allowance for variations and simplifications. Older pupils found considerable difficulty in speeding up their handwriting in secondary school, and frequently reverted to printing. In addition they felt that they were not permitted to take penlifts in the middle of long words. Penlifts make the act of writing more comfortable in that they allow the hand to move freely along the line without strain. With a relaxed hand the writing is more relaxed.

Continuous joins were necessary in the days of quill pens. Today they serve no real purpose. When children who have been taught to join every letter do stop, whether through discomfort or to hesitate over spelling, spacing separate letters can be a problem. If pupils are still using copybooks after the initial stages of joining a further difficulty arises. The copy book will be reproducing joined letters, or maybe penlifts before specific letters. The children are supposed to follow the copy and may be marked as incorrect if they are not doing exactly the same. But individual handwriting does not work in the same way.

Penlifts are not needed at exactly the same time by everyone or after a specific number of letters. They may depend on the complexity of movement within the letters, also on the particular combination of letters. The size and speed of the writer may alter the number of penlifts needed but there is an even more important factor to consider. In an efficient handwriting the form of the actual letters varies according to its position in the word, and perhaps to the preceding letter. It is easy to understand this in relation to the letter 's' where it is often abbreviated in the middle or end of a word. When it comes to a more complex letter like 'f' there are many different ways of forming and joining single and double ones that can be developed that are perfectly legible and usually more efficient than the full, basic form that will be appearing in a copybook.

Avoiding pain

Above all handwriting should not be painful for the writer. Over and beyond letterform aspects, the writer's body needs consideration right from the start. Wherever possible individual needs for adequate furniture, a choice of writing implements and a variety of lined papers should be provided to cater for those very differences that there will always be between individual children. Guidance needs to be given about where to place the paper. This should usually be to side of the hand that is used for writing. Any slant is optional. None of this advice should conflict with a new model, but all the good done by considering the comfort of the writing posture can be negated if the writer is under too much stress arising from the inability to produce prescribed letterforms. Such stress can distort posture, and in turn affect the letterforms by inhibiting still further the writer's ability to produce the desired strokes.

Flexible use of a handwriting scheme

It is this flexible and intelligent use of models that needs to be addressed by educationists. The way a new scheme is implemented is far more important that the model itself. An authority that allows for adequate in-service training can use such sessions to give teachers the confidence to use the new scheme in the best way for their pupils. If it is launched without adequate training then too often teachers put too much emphasis on the final product, the model, and too little emphasis on the method. A good authority will always be on the lookout for ways to improve the system that has been introduced. It does not inspect schools with the purpose of chastising teachers for lack of uniformity of handwriting that is displayed on the walls, but looks for real improvement in the flow and consistency of work that is in children's own exercise books. Any system should work on the principle that handwriting should be taught in such a way that it not only works for individuals but that they can enjoy the act of writing. Children need latitude in the levels that are demanded of them. If they are to write long stories then they cannot always be neat. Their letters cannot be exact copies of any model if they are to concentrate the maximum effort on recording ideas. Later on, if they are expected to take copious notes from a blackboard, there should not be shame but pride in having a fast efficient scribble for that purpose. Attitudes to writing need to change to suit today's needs.

CHAPTER 10

The National Curriculum

Some curriculum documents are very detailed. Some of the details are beneficial, when they result in dealing with the basic teaching of letters in a systematic way. Too rigid an approach, however, can sometimes be detrimental in such a subject that is as personal as handwriting. In addition, a slight error in a curriculum document in countries where teachers are required to follow it exactly, perhaps in a matter like paper position, or too didactic an attitude to penhold, can cause considerable problems. Liberal policies can also be found, as examples for the more child-orientated to follow. In Malaysia, while trying to find out why Malaysian students in British universities seemed to have such relaxed and efficient handwriting of a very high standard, I was delighted to be told by the head of curriculum development that they had no national model but concentrated on a systematic method. I was to see the impressive results of their national policy the following year when I was invited to comment on their specific problem of teaching in four different languages and three different writing systems. In the one Australian state, South Australia, with a liberal policy not yet tied to a formal model, I found instructions to teachers to encourage penlifts and not to teach the continuous cursive promoted by the copybook writers in the rest of the country. This enlightened instruction had been in force already for 15 years.

The national curriculum currently in use in Great Britain differs from those of other countries in that it only specifies goals and neither a specific model or method. This seems a good compromise, providing there is sufficient initial and in-service training to ensure that teachers know how to teach the subject. When the discussion document appeared in 1988 the main argument that I had was that the terminology was misleading. The problem of an imprecise terminology was mentioned in the introduction to this part of the book. I voiced my worries in an article in the Times Educational Supplement (17.2.89), quoting several of the goals:

Level 1
Begin to form letters but with little physical control over size, shape and/or *orientation* of letters

Level 2
Produce properly *orientated* and mainly legible upper and lower case letters in *one style* (*e.g. printed*)

Level 3
Begin to produce a clear and legible *cursive style*

Level 4
Produce a more fluent *cursive style* in independent work

Level 5
Produce clear and legible handwriting in both *printed* and *cursive styles*

The italics are my own.

My reservations were:
In levels 1 and 2: By using only the word 'orientation' the report gives the impression that letters with an incorrect movement are acceptable. A separate letter may face in the right direction and be legible, but unless it moves correctly it may never join properly.

In levels 2, 3 and 4: The words cursive styles and, even worse, printed and cursive styles are used. The Cox report suggests keeping to 'styles' such as print or cursive. Did it mean separate letters or joined letters? The word cursive means different things to different people, and print suggests the straight letters that many people believe to be partly to blame for the predicament of handwriting today. Whatever the terminology, the 'either print or cursive' idea is too rigid. Few efficient adult writers join more than five or six letters at a time without a penlift, so why should we expect children to do so? According to level 2 the resulting mix of separate and joined letters would not be approved of. Surely this report does not mean a return to the continuous looped cursives that were discarded over fifty years ago.

In addition I would have liked the words 'at increasing speed' to be added at level 5.

In the final document some of these anomalies were corrected but not all. The term 'recognisably formed' appeared, but only in level 2, and the accompanying illustration still showed only a b/d reversal. Just as important, the word 'joined up' replaced 'cursive' in level 3 – but the damage had already been done. The use of the word 'cursive' instead of the term 'joined-up', which is more familiar in this country, has lingered on. It has resulted in confusion and in my opinion some misinterpretation of the intentions of the curriculum document. Some unusually backward looking commercially produced models have come onto the market, along with some ill-informed statements to the press and others concerning the desirability of continuous cursive 'as recommended by the national curriculum'. All this stirred me into writing several articles explaining the issues involved in joining.

This section first appeared in Teaching Literacy: Balancing Perspectives, ed. Beard,1993.

TERMINOLOGY AND JOINS

To me the words 'cursive' and 'joined-up' mean the same, and I have used them both quite happily together in the past. That term 'cursive', however, seems to suggest something different to some people. They see it as more joined than joined-up, perhaps looped as well. Some people are going further and saying that this means that we should revert to versions of copperplate-based commercial cursives that went out of use in this country in the 1920s. To further justify these models those promoting them are saying that the French teach 'cursive' from the start. This is adding inaccuracy to misinterpretation. For many years it has been said, maybe half jokingly, that in the first term of school in every classroom in France all the children on any particular day will be learning exactly the same letter. French children have been taught for decades to learn their separate letters in this way, a whole page of one letter at a time, written on squared paper. Their separate letters have entry as well as exit strokes – maybe that is where the mistake arose. The French are finding that their secondary students are increasingly reverting to print because the continuous cursive that is the result of these letterforms disintegrates at speed. The whole matter of their national model has been under consideration for several years by a multi-disciplinary committee. Meanwhile Du Pasquier-Grall (1990) describes in some detail how the majority of French children actually learn to write 'Les lettres sont tracées *une à une* au debut (age 6-7 ans)' (my italics).

It is not advisable to compare national models without detailed knowledge of actual teaching methods within another country. The wording of the national curriculum should not be distorted and such misleading statements must be countered. They must not be allowed to be used to justify commercially lucrative, but not necessarily appropriate, handwriting models and to impose them on our children.

I went into more detail in another article (in the journal *Language and Learning*). Here I was concerned with reviewing a system that justifies continuously joined handwriting from the start by tying it to benefits to spelling. After explaining and illustrating what happens if young children are encouraged to join before the correct movement of basic letters has been established, the article went on to look at the reasons why the teaching of continuous cursive, without allowing for penlifts might not be of permanent benefit to children. From the point of view of teaching spelling, and for the same reason that of many teachers of children with learning difficulties, this may work with four or even five letter words. It is later on, when it may be too late to change the habit of continuous joining, that such a concept begins to work against pupils' best interests. Those who have joined every letter find it difficult not to join and even more difficult to space their letters if they do. In the same, way poor spellers find it confusing to try to work out long complex words within a continuously joined writing.

Looking at handwriting around the world and through the entire school age, it can be seen that there are considerable difficulties for people who have been so indoctrinated that they feel that all letters

This magnificent example shows the danger of encouraging children to join their letters before they have learned the correct movement (point of entry and direction of stroke) of separate letters. Reproduced from Sassoon (1990) *Handwriting: The Way to Teach it.*

should be joined all the time. Generations of Americans and other nationalities can demonstrate the deficiencies of continuous cursive training when it comes to speeding up handwriting and developing the personal joins and penlifts that lead to an efficient hand. Then there are the practical consequences of continuous cursive which can be set against an historic background. The beautiful copperplate writing, forerunner of continuous cursive, was written with a pointed quill or steel nib, held in such a way that all the weight was on the little finger so that the pen could glide along easily. Try writing that way with an unsupported wrist, using a modern pen. Our pens, and the way we write with our hand supported on the table, demand that in order to write easily at speed, and particularly under pressure, we need to have penlifts every so often during long words. Try writing a word like 'extraordinary' or 'uncoordinated' without lifting your pen. Children deserve to be told that, despite the many advantages of joining their letters, they should only join when comfortable. If

The disadvantages of continuous cursive often show up when it is too late for writers to alter their accustomed movent. Reproduced from Sassoon and Briem (1984).

articles please get

articles please get

David's problem was that he had been taught to join up every letter every time. He had rebelled and gone back to printing.

comunity community

com mu nity

Not only did the continuous joining distort his letters and slow him down, but it muddled up his spelling too.

independent indep

inde ind independent

He was much happier when he was shown how to take a break in the middle of long words. It helped both his writing and his spelling.

not, then many of the best of them feel guilty when taking a penlift, and try to disguise this, often with a false joining stroke.

A general trend towards unjoined letters in secondary school can be seen all round the world. This is equally evident in countries like the USA and continental Europe where strict cursive models have been followed, and in Great Britain where a perhaps too relaxed an attitude to joins has been apparent in recent years. If we want to meet students' needs then we must learn to read the signs and adapt any didactic rulings that may be based on outdated implements or models, making allowance for the changed usage of writing and the emphasis on speed.

Assessment

Whether for those involved in a planning national curriculum or those evaluating written work in any particular school or district, the question of the assessment of handwriting will arise eventually. I had to face this issue when I was asked to write a chapter in a book that used previously written examples of creative writing from a massive national sample. It had been gathered from many thousands of children. The task itself forced me to focus on matters that I had previously avoided – and I did not find this easy. I would not expect everyone to agree with my method of assessment. The huge variations in the style and standard of handwriting helped me to reach certain conclusions. Those conclusions are of help to me in a task that I perform for a major pen manufacturer when I assess several thousand entries for an annual handwriting competition. On those occasions I add the judgement of 'consistency' to the more measurable factors that follow.

Many judgements concerning handwriting are subjective. What one person likes, another hates. What one person finds easy to read another finds illegible. It often depends on what you are used to, what your expectations are, and even what your own handwriting is like. Quality is difficult to assess and a judgement is likely to be unrealistic unless the task is appropriate to a qualitative judgement. It is not realistic to judge the quality of the handwriting in a piece of creative work, unless the quality or amount of content is taken into account. When copying a final draft, with unlimited time and no other worries such as spelling or grammar to contend with, most children can lift the level of their handwriting. As for speed tests, all they prove is that certain children wrote so many letters in such a time on such a day in specific circumstances. The task that they had been given might or might not have any relevance to what they have to do in class, so the results may not reflect realistically their normal performance. Both qualitative and speed norms are unsatisfactory, and often unfair to children, yet some researchers seem to delight in producing them.

Assessing joins

So how can we assess handwriting in any purposeful way? Perhaps we should start, in any particular instance, by deciding what is important. If joins are important then they can be counted, so can the intermediate stages such as whether the letters touch, but do not join, and whether the letters have exit strokes at the baseline or still finish abruptly on the baseline as in print script letters. An accurate count of joins might reveal how well a school's policy of encouraging joining is working out. It could reveal the effects of different models or methods. This would not mean that such a count should be used to prove that there is an optimum degree of joining for all children. Perhaps the real benefit of such group assessments would be the highlighting of personal and permissable differences between and within the writing of individuals. Much could be learned from comparing examples of fast and slow handwriting, looking at the difference in the total joins when writing at speed, also at differences in the types of join. This is using assessment more for the instruction of the researcher. The most beneficial assessment for individual children compares their developing work against examples written at various earlier stages.

In this particular exercise visual analyses of such matters as size and slant were proposed, with the intention of demonstrating that a sliding scale of such elements could be produced, but the cut-off point would always be subjective. In this way some of the smallest handwriting might be seen to be among the most legible. It could also be demonstrated that handwriting which has a slight backwards slant, rather than the preferred upright or forward angle of the copybook writers, is not necessarily any the less legible.

Assessing the incorrect movement of letters

In my view the most useful overall measure is how many children in any particular group have incorrect movements. Our alphabet has evolved to work best with a conventional point of entry and direction of stroke. Handwriting cannot be speeded up or joined and remain legible unless the basic movement of the letters is correct. The hand movements involved in producing and proceeding from one letter to the next (whether on or off the paper) be inefficient and lack the rhythm that is needed for a smoothly flowing handwriting.

A national sample has certain advantages over one taken in a relatively small district, but there were other problems inherent in this particular one that made valid analyses or assessments difficult. It is sometimes almost impossible to detect the movement of certain letters without watching the writer in action. Within these limitations a simple analysis was worked out. The total of faults detected would, in reality, be much higher. Usually the worst writers wrote the shortest stories and few children used all 26 letters. Even so, without many incidences of the less familiar letters such as 'q', 'z' or even 'j', the total of children showing one or more movement faults was a clear indication of the need for more intensive teaching. One hundred of each age group were scrutinised, using equal numbers of boys and girls, from the same proportion of urban and rural schools, distributed throughout the country. At seven years old 54% showed movement faults, some in as many as six letters. At eight 48% produced discernable faults, still showing pupils with individual faults in five or six letters. At nine although the incidence of children with movement faults had fallen to 36% (with one boy producing his work on a word-processor), several of these children still showed four or five different faults. It must be suspected that in a formal exercise using all 26 letters would have produced worse figures. It was not hard to assess which letters were the most frequent offenders overall:

> 'f' with 59 discernable instances,
> 'd' with 53,
> 'o' with 37
> 'a' with 33

The conclusion was that an analysis of movement faults was likely to be more useful in the early stages of handwriting than any other attempt at a legibility assessment. This is because it would show the incidence of the main cause of illegibility in more mature handwriting. It would also have the advantage of pointing out the importance of a teaching method that stresses the correct movement of basic letters.

It is this final advice that was proffered to our national curriculum council who are still searching for a valid means of assessing the early stages of handwriting.

This section is based on a presentation made to the National Curriculum Council in November 1992.

HANDWRITING IN THE NATIONAL CURRICULUM

Then suddenly one day I was invited to meet those responsible for planning the revised English curriculum, which includes handwriting. I was asked to prepare a presentation that looked at the goals and markers of progression, in ten stages, from school entry to school leaving. Tests were proposed to take place at seven, eleven and fourteen. If there were going to be formal tests then it seemed that they would have to be closely linked to the goals from the start. In November 1992 I tried to set out a coherent plan to deal with the situation as it stands at this moment in our country. It was more or less as follows.

We need balanced and informed goals that describe precisely the essentials in such a way as to compel teachers to address the key issues at each stage. The goals themselves must lead to valid and practical criteria by which children's progress can be assessed. These tests should also be able to indicate the success or otherwise of any particular school's policy. It is vital that any written examples that may appear in documents that are meant to advise teachers about testing should reflect the principles behind the policy.

We need a new approach. We should start by looking at the school leavers' goal. The final attainment level should be decided first.

Level 10.
A mature, personal and efficient handwriting flexible enough to be adapted to the requirements of further education or the work-place.

Then we should consider how to teach from the beginning to ensure that these goals are met. We have a responsibility to take into account that the usage of handwriting has altered. It is increasingly needed for more personal tasks, like note-taking. These tasks necessitate a fast efficient handwriting. This need is best met by encouraging a consistent personal hand, rather than close adherence to a specific model. This in turn requires a change of attitude by all concerned, so that people value personal differences in handwriting from early on, instead of trying to eliminate them. The tasks that have in the past required that handwriting should be uniform are increasingly being undertaken by the keyboard.

Handwriting is a multi-disciplinary skill and we need a multi-disciplinary approach. Educational aspects, physiological aspects and letterform aspects all need informed consideration. Although, as I understand it, the National Curriculum Council does not intend to dictate the details of method, the markers of progression and any related tests must be informed by such principles.

The educational background is already set by the other areas of the English curriculum; handwriting is expected to be used from the very early days, so any teaching method must of necessity be systematic and efficient, dealing with the essential movement of letters. It must also impart effective writing strategies for such matters as posture, penhold and paper position. The special needs of left-handers must be understood, and extra care taken with children who may have motor or perceptual problems.

Against this background, levels of achievement can be suggested, on the understanding that radical alterations of those previously set is not wanted at this time.

Levels 1 to 3 – In the Primary School
Level 1
Pupils should begin to form letters with some control over size and shape, with emphasis on the correct point of entry and direction of the strokes that make up our letters (i.e. the movement of letters). They should begin to clump letters into words showing that they have an understanding of the task of handwriting.

Level 2

Pupils should be able to produce legible upper and lower case letters (or the terms could be more handwriting-orientated 'Capital Letters and Small Letters'), and use them appropriately.

They should be able to produce consistent letterforms, with the correct movement, with clear ascenders and descenders, and appropriate height differentials. Emphasis should be on baseline exit strokes in readiness for joining. Spontaneous joins along the baseline should be encouraged as well as joins within short words and common letter combinations.

They should be able to space letters and words appropriately.

Level 3

Pupils should know how all the letters join by now, and they should be able to demonstrate that they have attained a certain degree of joining in their everyday handwriting. They should be able to join all the letters in short words, or in common letter combinations. However, penlifts are beneficial during the writing of longer words, so children should not be penalised for taking them.

In my opinion these aims cannot be reached without:

Efficient letters that join easily and need no alteration in movement between the ages of five and sixteen – i.e. letters with integral exit strokes at the baseline, but no entry strokes.

A systematic method that teaches the correct movement of letters in stroke related families.

Informed teaching of handwriting posture from the beginning, leading to good writing strategies for paper-position, penhold etc., with special attention paid to the requirements of left-handers.

An understanding that letters that lead to early joining will not be as conventionally neat as print script.

An understanding that the production of handwriting is linked with other literacy skills, so that poor spelling or hesitations and tension in other areas will be reflected in children's handwriting performance.

Levels 4 to 6 – In the Junior School

The next three attainment levels are concerned with the years between eight and eleven, when the next tests are planned. These levels must be progressive, but I am suggesting a more lenient level 4. This is to ensure that children with problems can be tested with tasks appropriate to their age, but with the recognition that some eleven-year-old's, for whatever reason, may still have difficulty with joining their letters and speeding up their handwriting.

Level 4

The pupils should demonstrate the ability to write clear separate letters, all demonstrating the correct movement, for labelling, as well as consistent capital letters for headings.

To produce an everyday handwriting and to be able to improve on the quality of this when requested to copy a text in a slower more careful hand.

Within everyday handwriting the pupil should be able to form all the letters with a correct movement. The letters should show that the pupil has an understanding of height differentials and letter and word spacing appropriate to the size and style of handwriting.

Within everyday handwriting the pupil should show, through the presence of exit strokes, that he or she is progressing towards joined letters. It would be expected that some letters would join spontaneously in faster handwriting.

Level 5

Pupils should be able to write clear separate letters for labelling, as well as consistent capital letters for headings.

Pupils should be joining by standard joins in their everyday handwriting in short words and common letter strings. Penlifts are desirable at least every five letters, and pupils should not be penalised for taking them.

Pupils should be able to speed up their writing when necessary. There should be a marked difference in the standards of special occasion handwriting, classroom handwriting and fast personal handwriting. At all levels of handwriting the movement of all letters should be correct, and the height differentials and letter and word spacing should be appropriate to the style of handwriting.

Level 6

Pupils should display a competence within all the different types of handwriting already listed. Within special occasion, ordinary classroom and fast handwriting they should demonstrate that they are confident in an appropriate level of joining i.e. within words of up to five letters and within common-letter strings of up to five letters.

In their faster writing they should show that they have confidently broken from the taught model and developed a consistent personal handwriting. It is important that they should not be penalised for beginning to develop the shortcuts and personal joins that will help their handwriting to mature and enable it to speed up further in secondary school.

What should not be left uncorrected at any age

It is to the benefit of the writer that, at any age when it is noticed, the incorrect movement of basic letters should be pointed out and an explanation given as to precisely why it will benefit the writer to alter that movement.

Writing posture

Although this is not being given prominence in the curriculum document, it must be mentioned that these are the years when informed teachers can give pupils help in correcting any postural faults. This includes finding pens and penholds to suit individual hands and handwriting. Many pupils need help in these years to understand the effect of paper position and body posture on the freedom of arm and hand movements necessary for fast writing. In turn teachers and pupils together will begin to understand the effects of these factors on the written trace. Children seldom experience pain from awkward writing postures before the age of eleven. However if such postures continue into the later years, tension, pain and cramp are the increasingly frequent consequences. Left-handers are at particular risk, as are those who are unusually tall or short for their age. The height of their chairs and tables are often inappropriate and they are seldom able to sit in a comfortable position to write.

Self-criticism

An ability to judge the good and less good features of handwriting is a prerequisite of progress. There are plenty of ways of teaching self-criticism without destroying pupils' confidence, e.g. giving equal praise for the discerning of the least good letter in a set, as is given for choosing the best. The years between seven and eleven are ideal for developing such discrimination in a positive way.

Development of a personal style

When pupils have been taught to follow a strict model, it is important that they are encouraged to break from it before they leave the junior school. They may need assistance to find the shortcuts within the style and proportions of their own handwriting. All this requires informed teaching.

Levels 7 to 10 – In the Secondary School

In these years it is not easy, or necessarily constructive, to divide what is a natural progression towards a mature handwriting into three levels. However the National Curriculum requires that this is done, so an attempt must be made.

Level 7

Pupils should be able to write fluently and consistently in a personal style using a balanced level of joining, i.e. letter strings of up to five letters, but exhibiting penlifts during the writing of longer words as desired.

Pupils should be able to use flexibly the different types of letterforms and handwriting suited to the different tasks that will now confront them at school. In addition to those developed in primary school, they require: a careful but mature writing such as might be used on a final draft of an important letter or finished project work, with the movement, height differentials, spacing and joining criteria as already stated; and they require faster letters that enable them to take notes in class.

Pupils should be able to present their work on the page in a way appropriate to the task, beginning to use presentation and page layout to facilitate the organisation of their work.

Level 8
In addition to previous levels of handwriting pupils now should be able to produce faster but still legible letters, suitable for external examinations, with the movement, height differentials and joining criteria as previously mentioned. Layout has become even more important and pupils should demonstrate that they understand that layout and the division of text are important to the appearance of the page and the appreciation of their written work.

Level 9
In addition to previous levels of handwriting pupils should be able to produce very fast handwriting, suited to more intensive note taking. This level of writing needs to be legible only for the writer, and could be described more as a personal scribble.

   Pupils should be able to write for considerable periods under pressure without experiencing physical discomfort.

   The last point accentuates the need for teachers to find out those who suffer needless discomfort when writing fast, or for a certain length of time. They can then advise those pupils on any change of writing posture or strategy that might be necessary to alleviate pain. This brings us back to the criteria for a school leaver's handwriting, stated at the beginning of this section.

Level 10.
A mature, personal and efficient handwriting flexible enough to adapt to the requirements of further education or the work-place.

Tests and testing techniques at the age of seven
A thorough test of the skill of handwriting, separate from other skills, should be within a copying task rather than in a spontaneous piece of writing. Such a test might consist of several short sentences, in order to include all the letters of the alphabet in appropriate words and phrases for this age group. A variety of joins are likely to be present. This written task should enable three valid and easily recorded judgements to be made.

1   Letters with the correct movement
2   Letters with appropriate height differentials
3   Letters joining, or ready to join

It is not easy to discern the movements of all letters from previously written samples and unrealistic to expect teachers to watch each child in action during a written test. Part of the training for teachers to carry out this test could be the requirement that they observe some problem writers in action and tabulate their movement faults.

Each judgement could be in three grades.

For movement (from lowest to highest mark)

1 Four or more letters discernable with an incorrect movement.

2 Up to three letters with an incorrect movement.

3 All letters with the correct movement.

For height differentials (from lowest to highest mark)

1 Ascending and descending strokes that are inappropriately positioned in relation to other letters.

2 Ascenders and descenders that are appropriately positioned in relation to other letters but are not sufficiently pronounced or are confusing in other ways.

3 Adequate ascenders and descenders appropriate in relation to other letters.

For joining three stages can be observed and counted if desired

1 A majority of separate letters without exit strokes

2 A majority of separate letters with exit strokes ready to join with a few spontaneous baseline joins.

3 Joined strings of letters up to four or five letters long. Pupils should not be penalised for the presence of penlifts in words of more than three or four letters.

Consistency of slant and size are also important, but at this time they are not as important as the three criteria already mentioned. They are also more difficult to assess for testing.

If testing should be undertaken in an example of creative writing, those children with problems, who are most likely to fall into the lowest category, will probably produce the shortest examples of written work. They will not be likely to include the less commonly used (and frequently incorrectly written) letters such as 'x', 'z', 'j', 'q' or even 'p' and 'j'. In effect they will provide the smallest selection of the letters of the alphabet. Spontaneous writing should be used with care when testing handwriting because there is always a risk of invalidating any quantitative judgement of movement errors.

Tests at the age of eleven

These tests could be constructed to include separate letters within a labelling task, capital letters within a heading task, followed by a simple text to be attempted in a slow careful hand, an everyday hand, and a fast personal hand to demonstrate that the pupil has begun to break away from the taught model. Any mark could be graded according to the number of tasks that are successfully carried out, with satisfactory movement of letters, height differentials and spacing (and joins where appropriate).

Tests at the age of fourteen

In the unlikely event of a formal test being needed at this age it should be of a text to be repeated in the various types of handwriting described in the levels of attainment. Such a test should not be timed against a norm but a comparative speed element could be included, within the student's own examples. This would illustrate that they understand the need for flexibility, and that the speed of their writing will reflect the task and influence the conventional neatness of their handwriting.

Any judgement would have to take into consideration that this is an age of experimentation and handwriting is likely to alter frequently as the teenage writer matures. Any estimation of a pupil's ability to lay out and present work at a satisfactory level would be better to come from observing class or project work.

...But this is not the end of the matter; the discussions continue.

Retraining a Stroke Patient

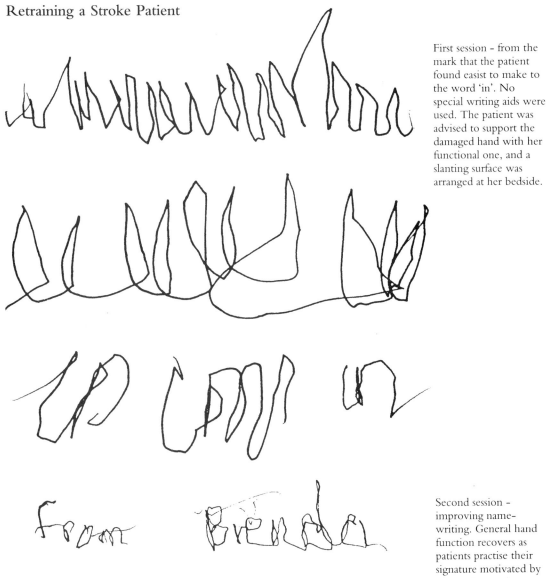

First session – from the mark that the patient found easist to make to the word 'in'. No special writing aids were used. The patient was advised to support the damaged hand with her functional one, and a slanting surface was arranged at her bedside.

Second session – improving name-writing. General hand function recovers as patients practise their signature motivated by an ever improving visible trace.

CHAPTER 11

The Therapeutic Aspects of Handwriting

Diagnosis and explanation

During the years that I have been looking at handwriting problems I have altered radically both my techniques and my whole attitude to the situation. I have always stressed that a clear diagnosis is vital, and without sufficient understanding to give the patient an equally clear explanation, no exercises are likely to help. I tried to explain my diagnostic techniques in the slim teachers' book to *Helping Your Handwriting,* (Nelson 1986), refusing to reduce the necessary observations to a simple checklist, but showing ways of observing and tabulating the different possible causes of problems. For myself, I found any formal diagnostic technique less and less effective. The more I took the attitude with patients that I knew nothing and that the they probably could reveal the specific problems if asked the right questions, the more satisfactory the results. Of course these questions were informed and dependent on observations that began as soon as the patient entered the door, even before we shook hands. This technique became necessary as increasingly I realised that complex handwriting problems seldom had anything to do with the ability to form letters. The reason becomes clearer when instead of looking for ways to improve the legibility of the written trace for the benefit of the reader, you begin to consider the handwriting as the clue to the underlying causes of the patient's distress.

'What kind of handwriting do you like?' is a question that I try to avoid answering. Instead I describe the kind of writing that it most distresses me to see. That is where there are certain words or passages that show that the writer is quite able to produce mature, well spaced, consistent letters, whereas in other parts of the same page all kinds of errors are evident – of movement, in the usage of capitals, in slant in spacing and above all in the pressures of the writing. This signals to me that something serious is getting in the way of the writer who can write adequately in ideal circumstances.

The challenge is then to find out what is getting in the way. The explanation to the patient may not solve the situation in school, at home or at work that caused such tension as to distort the handwriting. A sample of their own writing in a relaxed atmosphere, however, can be a great comfort to those who thought that their handwriting was beyond repair.

Remedial education

In the educational field, a whole industry has grown up independent of the school system. The individuals (or tutors) concerned earn their living from dealing with learning difficulties. They may know how to deal with spelling and reading problems but seldom have the knowledge to deal with the implications of handwriting. Many such people are unwilling to accept that the pupil, with the right diagnosis and encouragement, is the best person to help him or herself. Their training as well as their inclination is far too often to try to interfere with the style of the child's handwriting. In so doing they attempt to build a dependence on themselves and the 'safety' of their imposed style. I fight this attitude wherever and whenever I can, and stress the importance of praise rather than uninformed criticism. To attack people's handwriting is to attack them themselves. To interpret the written trace is a most valuable diagnostic aid. But there is a problem. There is no course of training to follow. An understanding of all the issues involved can only come from close observation and an open mind.

For several years now I have preferred to lecture more about handwriting as a diagnostic aid than to give advice about remedial exercises. It is not always easy to make therapists, for instance, understand that the diagnosis and explanation may be sufficient, and that no further therapy is needed. This problem was illustrated clearly in the chapters concerning adult writer's cramp. I put some ideas together for the journal *Therapy*, and others for the journal *Speech Therapy in Action*. Some excerpts from them are reproduced here to illustrate certain points that have not been covered elsewhere in this book. There are also some implications relevant to adult literacy that were highlighted in an article in the *Times Educational Supplement*.

Adult literacy

Problems do not go away, and can be compounded under layers of increasing frustration and tension. I tried to point out some of the implications for adult literacy teachers in an appropriately named article; 'It is never too late' in the *Times Educational Supplement* (23.11 84). Students who come to 'basic skills' classes often have multiple problems, so it is difficult to know which to tackle first. I explained that, unless the pupil specifically asked for it, handwriting might not be the best starting point. This is despite the possibility that, on a purely mechanical approach, it might be easier to solve than other deficiencies in literacy skills. Providing these adults can write at all they can at least read their own script and put something down on paper. To attempt to change it too soon might destroy even that shred of confidence. I explained the desirability of any improvement being carried out within the personal style of the student, having been witness to some distressing teaching of the 'why don't you try to write nicely like me' type. Above all I tried to explain that those with literacy problems would reflect their insecurity and sometimes their immaturity too in their handwriting until they became more articulate and gained more skill in spelling and grammar. Looking at it that way, some faults might be self-correcting as confidence built up. Whatever the state or stage of handwriting, praise would always work better than criticism.

Handwriting therapy

Occupational and physiotherapists as well as speech therapists are increasingly having to develop methods of dealing with problems that were traditionally solved at school. Not having an effective handwriting is a real deprivation whether you are a handicapped child, or, for instance, an adult recovering from a stroke. Our approach to a problem is obviously influenced both by our training and our experience. Physiotherapists who might best deal with the hand aspect often feel, with some justification, that there are more important 'daily living' skills to deal with. They may not realise that retraining the hand to write with a simplified technique may, because of its visual feedback and importance to the individual, provide patients with just the motivation to work at improving their precision grip. This can result in a faster return to using a knife and fork and manipulating other everyday objects.

Neurological impairment

Much of my early work was undertaken at a local stroke club. There were fallacies to expose – such as the idea that either capital letters or childish separate print would be easier for stroke patients to learn. Repositioning the pen is the most difficult job to do with a shaky hand. Most adult patients will have retained the image and movement of the letters so, unless the patient shows a preference for writing in capital letters, ordinary handwriting and joins should be encouraged.

There were some light-hearted solutions, such as when some of the elderly patients disclosed that their hands felt cold because of poor circulation. This brought to mind a cartoon I had once seen of mediaeval scribes wearing mittens. The next week I brought mittens for the patients and indeed warmer hands made writing and retraining easier.

There were practical suggestions such as the use of a slanting writing surface. Able-bodied writers profit from this too, but for the disabled, specially those with a tremor, it is even more important that the whole arm is supported. It can make a dramatic difference to how those with a tremor steady the hand and control the pen. A piece of board resting on a couple of books provides a simple solution if nothing else is available. For those in wheelchairs, resting the board on the lap is even better. It gives the writer a chance to set the best height and angle for themselves, and it avoids the problem of chair arms that get in the way. In hospitals, therapists can usually find fully adjustable tables. They should make use of them, allowing patients to experiment to find an appropriate height and angle. Some patients with severe tremors may manage best standing up with their legs braced apart and the table almost upright. After all, this is the way that clerks wrote a century ago.

Many patients give up all hope of writing as a result of various conditions, but there are often techniques to help them if you are ingenious and confident enough to devise them. In degenerative diseases a change from one type of pen to something else that works more smoothly can prolong the ability to write. In addition the writing strategy may be altered to make use of less damaged muscles. A multiple sclerosis patient, for example, whose fingers and wrists were no longer functional, learned to write again using more of a shoulder movement – and soon found that she had a more legible script than before her illness.

Penhold

You will need an informed and inventive attitude to penhold. All kinds of penholds have been in use in past centuries, and you will need the confidence not only to experiment but to instil confidence in your patients. Much has already been written on this subject in other parts of this book. An open mind is needed towards the writing implement as well as the penhold when working with the disabled. You do not need to invest in expensive commercial writing aids. The patient's 'other hand' is usually a better and more sensitive support than the heavy stabilising weights often suggested in therapists' manuals. As for pen handles to suit damaged hands, there is usually a commonsense solution using materials to be found in any home.

Letters

The approach to letters is important, and the copybook approach (using material designed to teach schoolchildren) is not to be recommended. Whatever mark the patient is able to make should be the starting point. It is essential that the first session be optimistic and within the range of the most damaged patient. What you, the therapist, might impose in the way of an exercise may involve a movement that you can do easily, but it could be the movement that is most difficult for any particular patient. Start from the patient's own trace, however crude, and work up from there. This provides the best opportunity for refining and improving it, and progressing towards letters that will work for individual patients in their altered circumstances.

Signature

For an adult the signature is almost as important a daily living skill as making a cup of tea. If you are unable to produce a signature you are dependent on others to conduct your business affairs. This is particularly upsetting to those who have previously been independent, perhaps holding executive positions. Legibility is not essential for a signature but consistency is. Altogether this makes a signature one of the first goals when retraining a patient to write. It has an added bonus. The motivation is so intense that patients will spend hours practising. It is as effective in the retraining of a precision grip as the usual practice of asking patients to pick up buttons from one receptacle and replace them in another – and much more satisfying. A pack of 'thank you' cards, ready to be signed, has stood me in good stead with stroke patients and provided them with added incentive to write.

With all of this in mind, the skill should slowly return. In retraining handwriting with the vital motivation and visible feedback that it entails, the hand gains strength and agility for other daily living skills.

Attitudes

There needs to be a change in attitude concerning the retraining of damaged hands rather than encouraging the use of the non-preferred hand. The case of the man who was still using his left hand, because it pleased his therapist, long after his right one was functional, taught me a useful lesson. The examples that he produced illustrated the point that changing hands will alter the letters and is seldom as effective as the original hand. Some patients confessed that their altered handwriting no longer seemed representative of themselves, while others will have persistent difficulties with the direction of writing when using the left hand.

When the damaged hand can never again be functional, with sufficient motivation it should be quite easy to train afresh, and I tried to explain it this way: the writer will need new strategies for writing. The paper must first go over to the side of the new writing hand. The favourite fountain pen that was used with the right hand, and became adjusted to a right-handed slant, will be a disadvantage to the left hand. A modern fibre-tip which glides easily over the surface of the paper usually proves much better. The resulting letters will look different, but that is to be expected, and simplifications to certain complex letters are to be encouraged.

Be realistic in your aims. You cannot expect to persuade intelligent adults, faced with the problem of a severe tremor, that their writing after a stroke is, or ever will be, identical to that before their illness. You can, however, explain how a relaxed and positive approach produces the best possible writing in the circumstances.

Deformities of the hand

When dealing with those with hand deformities there are implications beyond the mere act of writing. They can help us to understand how the hand that writes can affect the writer's attitudes to his or her whole body. Nothing about this side of my work has yet been published, although slides of the patients mentioned here have often been shown at medically-orientated in-service sessions. Once again, informed discussion has added to an understanding that had previously been based only on a few cases.

I have not specialised in any way in advising those with hand deformities. A lack of medical knowledge once made me feel rather inadequate, until I realised how little those with medical qualifications knew about the mechanics of handwriting. With children who had been born with a handicap there seldom seemed to be any trouble. From birth such children had become ingenious in adapting to strategies that enabled them to make the best of their condition. Any suggestions that I would make about penhold, for instance, were always seized upon and experimented with gleefully. Some people seem to think that now that computers enable even the severely disabled to communicate, there is little purpose in encouraging the use of handwriting. I learned an early lesson from a five-year-old with a condition called arthrogryposis. His hands had no flexibility, but he could already manipulate the computer with dexterity, using his two little fingers. However, he had a burning desire to write like everyone else. From some photographs that were sent to me, a solution appeared to be impossible, but when we met, his eager expectation meant that something had to be done. With two opposing, but inflexible hands, a two-handed technique seemed to be the only answer. He took to this idea straight away, and some six years later, with slight interlacing of his fingers to facilitate speed, this young man finds handwriting no more difficult than any other pupil. In his particular case using a computer might not be as fast as his own writing.

Another child, who had thalidomide-like deformities (a right hand attached to the shoulder and a left one to the elbow) had already developed an efficient penhold with her left hand. She placed the pencil between the web of her fourth finger and little finger (I have since seen this penhold in a carving of an Egyptian scribe of the second century BC). She did not need my help, unless it was to show her how a slanted desk helped her posture. With such instructors, I would be remiss if I did not pass on to others this inventive attitude to severe problems.

In cases of acquired deformities, however, other forces seem to be at work. A boy who had suffered a stroke was brought to me. He was having problems trying to write with his left hand. He held his right hand behind him, and said that it was his enemy. His friends at school called him the one-armed bandit which upset him. All this was puzzling as the boy displayed no signs of a limp. His medical notes disclosed that he had received therapy for his leg, but not for his hand. It seemed essential that he should not reject his right hand. It also seemed logical that the hand should respond to treatment in the same way that his leg had – but I see patients only once. A packet of chocolate biscuits provided the motivation for him to use his damaged hand. He was allowed to take the first one with his left hand but any subsequent ones had to be taken with the right one. It worked, and from there it was a short step to show him that, with practise, he would be able to write again with his right hand. To write in his case was important, but to regain confidence in his whole arm was probably an even more important step.

This rejection of a hand arose again in the case of a child born without a right thumb. Her index finger had been repositioned surgically to create the opposition so necessary for a precision grip. The child was not using the repaired hand, and, more ominously, was trying to keep it out of sight. Like the previous patient she was having difficulties writing with her left hand. In the boy's case the problem was mostly dealing with the left-to-right direction of strokes. In this case the left hand did not function efficiently. The girl said that she could not write with her 'new thumb', and did not like it – a negative attitude, although understandable. Perhaps her parents or teachers were being too protective, because they were not encouraging her to use it. With an unconventional penhold and a pen of her choice she was soon writing happily.

After a few minutes she was switched to a conventional tripod grip, which not only worked comfortably and efficiently, but minimised the slight deformity in a way that was credit to the surgeon's skill. Armed with the written example, and a great deal of praise, it is to be hoped that she would be encouraged to continue to write with her right hand, and to use it for other purposes as well.

Some conclusions

So the pieces of the puzzle gradually fit together. Take the writer's cramp patients in chapter 6 who explained how they felt when their body would not obey them, or described how the hand that refused to write soon refused to pick up a glass or perform other delicate tasks, as they lost faith in it. Then consider the motivation that signature writing can give to a stroke patient, and the advantages of retraining a damaged hand rather than changing to the other one. Then you return to the boy who said quite unnecessarily, for the lack of informed therapy, that his affected hand was his enemy. From these perspectives it is easier to judge the importance of encouraging the child with a surgically repaired hand to use it. The decision whether to use or ignore the hand that reflects your identity to the world (when it has the capacity to be functional) can have a serious consequences.

The following presentation sought to raise awareness both of the possibilities of using handwriting as a diagnostic aid, and of the therapeutic techniques that can be of assistance in particular in stressful situations. It was presented at the International Psychology Congress in Brussels in 1992, however similar presentations had been given to various medical and other psychological audiences in the past few years.

HANDWRITING AS AN INDICATOR OF STRESS

This paper was presented at the 25th International Congress of Psychology, Brussels 1992, part of the symposium *Children and Stress,* convened by Prof. W. Yule.

To me handwriting is not to be judged as good or bad, neat or untidy, as it all too often is by teachers, but as an indicator of the writer's condition at the moment of writing. Handwriting is the visible trace of a hand movement, a direct product of mind and body that leaves a permanent and portable record. The writer's posture is as valuable a diagnostic aid as the written trace itself. Mental stress from whatever cause will be transmitted via the hand and will affect and usually disrupt the written trace. In addition, actual physical stress can be caused by the act of writing. This is often the result of poor postural strategies, and can be exacerbated by the demands of speed or academic pressure, as well as by more serious trauma such as perhaps bereavement. Such stress can be so extreme as to cause pain which if ignored or mis-diagnosed may lead to the little-understood condition of writer's cramp.

I prefer not to work from previously written samples, as a graphologist might, but to observe writers in action, noting the head angle and eye movements, paper position and penhold, and perhaps the alterations in posture as the writer relaxes. There is a limit to what can be deduced from the writing alone. Any excess stress will be evident, but not the cause, so I use my observations to help me to ask the questions that so often reveal the real cause of supposed handwriting problems. I use the word 'supposed' on purpose because the first diagnostic decision must be whether there is anything wrong with the patient at all. Inadequate and inappropriate teaching has left far too many of our children without an adequate handwriting. They are then blamed for being unable to write. The downward spiral of frustration as well as the loss of confidence and tension involved in such emotions leads to further deterioration of the written trace. This invites further criticism and misery.

Handwriting reacts with other cognitive skills, so the stress involved, for instance, in an inability to spell can be evident in the written trace. Signs of tension and unhappiness from a multitude of reasons, from broken homes, bullying (from teachers as well as other pupils), bereavement, to fatigue or drug abuse – also gaps in early training from such disturbances as allergic hyperactivity or temporary hearing loss – all need to recognised and dealt with. Migraine and other debilitating conditions can produce inconsistent work that is often unjustly criticised. Physical problems such as 'clumsiness' or tremor obviously affect writing in ways that the writer is unable to control. It is unrealistic to expect such children to produce the neat handwriting expected by both parents and teachers who do not fully comprehend the implications of the written trace.

By the time that I see children and their handwriting the original cause may be hidden under layers of tension and frustration. Children do not willingly write badly; there is often a quite commonsense cause to the difficulty which is revealed by their trace or their writing posture or their subsequent answers to questioning. It is a challenge to diagnose the cause. An accurate diagnosis is essential, then the clear explanation to the patient which relieves them of the pressure of guilt and frustration. Any exercises come a poor third.

While observing the child in the act of writing it is possible to detect difficulties that can affect graphic as well as other skills. Directional, visual, and perceptual problems and 'wrong-handedness' all leave clues for the observant. Unconventional posture or penhold, bizarre errors in letterforms, so-called lapses of concentration should not be deplored, but be gently questioned. When such matters are brought out into the open children can often describe their own difficulties with such precision that we can all learn from their predicament. When these clues are ignored or misdiagnosed as dyslexia, dysgraphia, dyspraxia or any of the other common labels attached to the patients that I am sent, the effects on the unfortunate children concerned can be traumatic. Children labelled as slow learners, disruptive or underachieving, may be sent to inappropriate schools or special educational units. The misery and frustration often make the misdiagnosis a self-fulfilling prophesy.'

When I lecture about this aspect of my work the comments that follow are sometimes thought provoking. There are in an audience those who dismiss case studies as miraculous. That is insulting as well as unhelpful. There are also those who are more interested in my qualifications than in what I do. Then there are those who ask if I am training anyone up to follow my techniques, and there are those specialists who ask how I see in their patients what they cannot see. Finally there are those, who understandably, would like to carry out their own research into my technique and into the relief from tension that it seems to bring.

These questions are valid ones, and not so easy to answer. The only answer as to whether I am training anyone up to carry on my work must be rather open. All that I can do is to make people aware of the type of observations that they need to make, whatever branch of education and medicine (or letterforms) they work in. Each person brings to this task his or her own training and attitudes. Mine was founded in letterforms and I can only repeat that this is the most problematic of the disciplines that need to be understood on the way to handwriting diagnosis. It is unlikely that I would find anyone qualified in letterforms who would be able to devote enough time to this study, with little hope of finding funding for it. I have never had much faith in people who try to train others in their exact therapeutic methods. So much depends on the individual's personality, and the ever deepening understanding that comes from researching a particular subject. In this area, still on the fringe of science, I feel that anyone wanting to continue the kind of work that I have so enjoyed would be robbed of the initiative and excitement so necessary to continue, if they were too closely trained in my techniques – even if it were possible. There is another important factor to consider. The social and educational climate that influences handwriting changes so fast that a completely fresh view is probably a good idea every decade or so.

This also answers, to a certain extent, the question about what I see that others do not. I look at problems from such a different angle, with a different set of acquired observations, and without the inhibitions of a medical or therapist's training – and to be honest, without the responsibilities that these professions involve. I have never built up the defensive wall that those constantly dealing with medical cases are trained to develop. If my attitude is more informal and emotional then this may account for the extraordinary revelations that patients disclose to me, and why I sometimes find answers to problems that others do not see. There is a price to pay, however. This approach to patients of any age is very tiring, and much of their frustration and distress is absorbed by the end of a session. If I try to describe to those in the medical profession what I am, I like to take the description by a writer's cramp patient that appears on page 111 – 'a specialist in the mechanics of handwriting'. This is because no amount of expertise in diagnosing the causes of tension that distort both posture or handwriting is enough, without the ability to find different writing strategies for easing the resulting pain and physical tension, and to defuse the situation whenever necessary.

This leaves the matter of research into my techniques, and this is where I find considerable difficulty in separating my two responsibilities – to individual patients and to the furthering of knowledge. I must leave this to the future to resolve. I prefer not to have to make the decision to subject my patients to a research project. I feel that there is a considerable risk that, having them tested before and at intervals after treatment, would retard their recovery. Reminding patients of any age of their previous condition might destroy their new-found confidence and delay the return to unconscious, automatic writing.

This was written for me
by an elderly calligrapher
in Hong Kong. He told
me that it says 'Calligraphy
is the mirror of the mind'.
This quotation reflects the
feeling that unites the
different sections of the
book; that the written
trace, whether in an
everyday situation, a
scientific experiment or a
creative work, is in itself a
personal statement. It is an
indicator of the writer's
mood, health and
character, and as such its
individuality is to be
valued more than its
neatness or conformity to
any particular model. Its
variations should be a
source of wonder as well
as of study.

CHAPTER 12

Full Circle

This book ends as I have myself, by returning to the subject of letterforms and the art, rather than the science of handwriting. Once again, in this multi-faceted subject, this chapter reflects two different dimensions of letters; first how to interest children, then how to relate western lettering to the tradition of Chinese calligraphy.

Maybe there is another way forward to solve the lack of understanding about handwriting – through an understanding of the implications of more formal letterforms.

One of the earliest courses that I ran had been to teach teachers how to use the history of writing in course work as well as in a creative way. This never seemed to be understood unless I followed up with a day of practical work in individual schools. Over the years the enthusiasm of children coming to day or holiday lettering courses could not fail to impress (and sometimes shame) any adults present. Whether they wanted to try formal calligraphy or, better still, to create their own letterforms, their originality and feeling for letters was sometimes startling. Whether in suburban Kent or in the outback of Australia these children

The expressive realism of 'glue', by eleven-year-old John-Mark Zywko, won him first prize in a competition run by the Castle Museum, Norwich. From Sassoon and Lovett 1992.

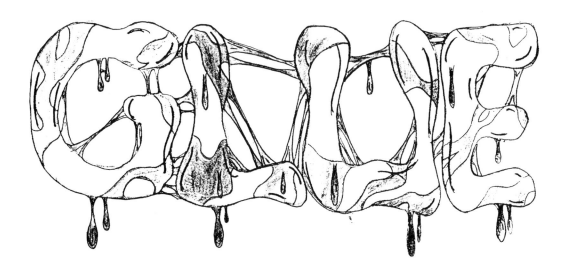

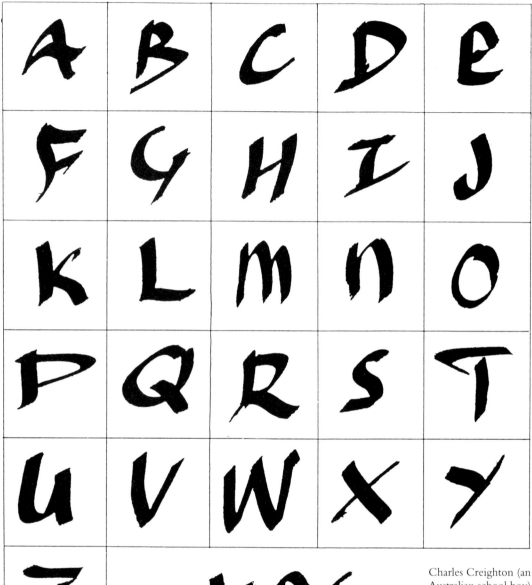

Charles Creighton (an Australian school boy) produced this personal set of letters. It was his first attempt and he consigned it to the wastepaper basket not realising its quality. Reproduced from Sassoon and Lovett (1992).

seemed to understand, and relate to their own handwriting from this exploration into the wider fields of letterforms. It seemed as if the creating of original letters came as naturally to young children as did drawing.

This gave me the idea that the children might teach their teachers, if only we could get this subject of lettering back into schools. Eventually it seemed important enough to revert to the 'art of writing' once again and get some of this material into book form.. With the help of Patricia Lovett, an ex-student of mine, and a quite exceptional one too, *Creating Letterforms* came to be written. The following excerpts are from various articles written at the time that this book was published. Here I am freer to make a more emotive appeal than when my presentation is more closely connected with the results of formal research. What effect this will have on the educational establishment remains to be seen.

Letters are important

Letters whether written, typed, printed or three dimensional are vital to communication. If written, they may influence the way people think about us, and in quite serious ways either open doors or limit progress. As far as handwriting is concerned, young children have for too long not been taught to write properly, yet are often blamed for their inability to produce a legible hand. In handwriting, if we fail, the untidy mess reflects back a sense of failure at us from the paper. Eventually the desire to write at all becomes atrophied. Reluctant writers fall further and further behind in their school work. To make your mark is a basic human need, and we do not fully understand the consequences of repressing this. Letters are a creative statement. We all produce our personally designed letters within our own handwriting so maybe it should all start with valuing the individuality of the written trace instead of what the teaching of handwriting has become – the copying of an arbitrarily imposed model.

I see all this as a part of the loss of awareness of the importance of letterforms in education and in our daily lives. In this age of computers, young children can become desk editors and call up letters on the keyboard. There is nothing wrong with that. What is disturbing is that our students, even at art school, all too often lack the visual perception and discrimination that comes through handling and using letters of all kinds. They have never had the opportunity to judge what is good or bad, either in the written or the printed page.

You can see the consequences of this neglect in the appalling spacing and letterforms that are printed out by the ever more technically perfect and expensive printers attached to school computers. It is too often evident in the poor typesetting of our newspapers as the traditional skills are no longer taught. We cannot depend on computers to make qualitative judgements. We must program and control them, not the other way around. In order to do this we need the knowledge and the experience of dealing with letters. If there is no way of learning later on, then the time to start is in early school days.

On the positive side letters are as creative a medium as painting or sculpture. Moreover letters are specially attractive to children who are imaginative enough to see and use their message. Every letter that is printed was once carefully designed with a specific purpose in mind. Letters have a life of their own, they give off messages that either impress and encourage us, or discourage and put us off. If typography is doing its job properly it should not be noticed. But in advertising we and our children need to be aware of how letterforms entice us and influence, via advertising what we buy or desire. We want to reawaken awareness to this fascinating and essential study. By encouraging letters in our schools we are giving children a most immediate form of self expression and opening up a subject that will be useful to them all their lives.

This brings us full circle – how today to interest children and their teachers in letterforms – how to give pupils of all ages the opportunity to handle and design their own letters without the need for specialised teaching. As I have built up this body of work, the interest, originality and confidence of the pupils has reassured me that they can teach their own teachers. If children are exposed to the excitement of letters they can communicate their special affinity with this medium, free from conventional adult model-orientated concepts of letters. Once the 'am I allowed to' attitude is dispersed, the children's true aptitudes and personalities show through. There are lessons for all of us here. I found children with no previous experience producing classical letterforms that were certainly not within their previous experience. Is there perhaps an inborn talent that is so seldom encouraged that it just never flowers? Anyone dealing with groups of children engrossed in such work cannot fail to be impressed by the way that it is often the least academically promising pupils who achieve success in free lettering, or perhaps replicating hieroglyphs. Perhaps the lesson is that to make one's mark is a human necessity. Look, for example, at the graffiti of the dispossessed and so-called delinquents in our midst. In their way they are works of art, however misplaced this art form may be on railway carriages or public property. How much better this talent might have been used, but in most education systems it is only conventional letters that are valued. In real life, however, and in the commercial world there is a great need for originality in letterforms. Not only have several generations been deprived of the possibility of learning this skill but industry has been starved of young people with the ability to design the letterforms needed for modern technology. It is not too late.

Whichever way you begin, it is easy to get children enthusiastic about letters. In fact the children's ideas and often amazing facility at producing original letterforms will soon draw any reluctant adults along in their wake From the work that Patricia Lovett and I have done with groups of children it seems as if there is boundless natural talent in this direction in young children. This seems to atrophy with age if it is not encouraged. Children are able to interpret the message that different typefaces or lettering suggests when adults, perhaps saturated with the variety around them, apparently no longer react.

What cannot be described in any book are the stories behind the illustrations – the expression on a disabled boy's face when he has designed a personal logo fit for printing on a tee-shirt, or the effect on a young teenager who has come to a weekend workshop, discovered letterforms, and designed his own personal 'typeface'. The consequences for both boys were far-reaching, in one case a growing self-confidence and improvement in all his written work, and in the other, even stronger several years later, a determination to develop this new-found talent and to aim for an art school training. All our children deserve this kind of experience.

THE PSYCHOLOGY OF WESTERN CALLIGRAPHY

This paper was presented at the 25th International Congress of Psychology, Brussels July 1992. It was part of a symposium entitled *Psychological Research of Calligraphy* convened by Prof. Henry Kao.

Quite recently I was invited to address the International Psychology Congress in Brussels on the subject of the psychology of western calligraphy. This posed quite a problem because it is unlikely that anyone has considered this subject in this particular way. The background to the symposium was to contrast any such work with that undertaken by Professor Kao, of the University of Hong Kong, on the psychology of Chinese calligraphy. He has specialised in isolating physiological differences that take place in the calligrapher during the act of producing Chinese characters, with a traditional brush or more modern pens. He records heartbeat, etc. to show such alterations.

Needless to say, a search revealed that no such work has been undertaken in the West, and although his work interests me, my own approach would have been fundamentally different to that of Professor Kao. To me the answers to any differences in calligraphy or the calligrapher lie in the traditions of the usage of letterforms, and maybe cultural and personal emotional attitudes, as well as in the innate differences between the two writing systems. The matters that I thought necessary to highlight were not those that could be proven, or are likely to be able to be reduced to a statistical table. The task of a scribe in whatever writing system requires similar levels of concentration, and the same bodily differences might well be discernable in the very few western scribes who nowadays attain the required level of competence, or attempt the serious professional tasks that require such levels of concentration. To me, such high-level nonetheless modest craftsmen as I know, might react somewhat quizzically to being wired to an machine. More seriously I personally find it difficult to see how such intervention would not interfere with the very automation and unconscious actions demanded by the task.

Anyhow, I took up the challenge and developed my theory as best I could and reproduce the brief text below. The presentation was divided into three parts:

1 The concept of the letter in Latin calligraphy within an historical perspective.

2 An analysis of the task of the scribe, and the possible physiological consequences of the deep concentration that it requires.

3 The psychological implications of the recent upsurge of calligraphy as a leisure pursuit rather than the essential craft that it once was.

A panel from the cover of *A History of Lettering* by Nicolete Gray (1986), illustrating lettering from illuminated manuscripts to neon signs. Reproduced here by kind permission of Phaidon Press.

True calligraphy transcends the replication of classic alphabets to allow the emotion of the meaning of the text to be transmitted via the hand to the paper. However, the concept of the written word within the Latin alphabet contrasts markedly with that of Chinese, Japanese or Arabic calligraphy, and to a certain extent, Hebrew.

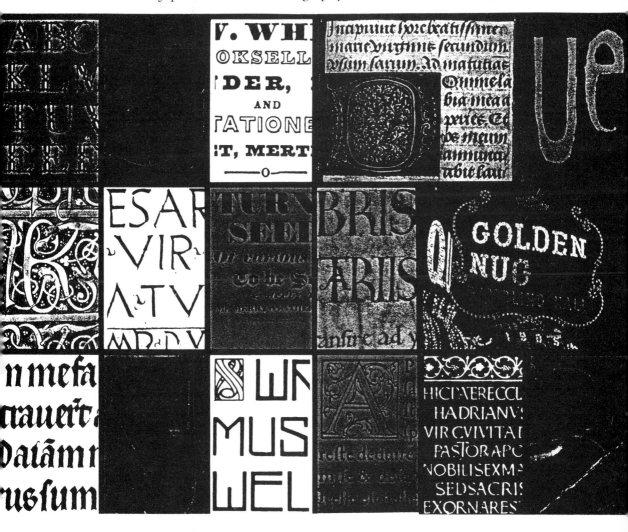

The Latin alphabet spread to a great extent with the growth of Christianity and consequently had to conform to the restraints of the church. With few exceptions, the message was all-important. (The exceptions illustrated with slides included the Lindisfarne Gospel 698 AD, and the Book of Kells 750 AD. Both of these famous manuscripts owe more to Celtic culture than to Christianity, and similar examples can be found all along the western fringe of Europe.) In later centuries the letterforms used in the body of the text were merely the means of delivering that message as clearly and economically as possible. Until recently the word 'lettering', rather than 'calligraphy', was used to describe handwritten text. The writer was termed a scribe but critical acclaim was reserved for the illumination, the decorated and often gilded embellishment usually completed by a specialist other than the writer of the text. There were, of course, a few exceptions.

Today a few scribes are developing a freer attitude to letterforms. The European calligraphers Wernher Schneider and Jovica Veljovitch are obvious choices. Others in the USA follow suit but much of their work tends to be derivative based on the few continental masters including, of course, the master of them all, Hermann Zapf, who have pioneered freer techniques. One girl, a working letterer, whose work is shown here, feels that she must call her work 'expressive calligraphy' to differentiate it from the more formally set out attitudes and work. The judgements of current work, as illustrated in exhibition choices, shows clearly what is still valued. The most praised layouts are carefully planned. The text, colours and headings carefully balanced. Perfect letters seem still to be more valued than any emotion that might be expressed by them.'

The audience was presented with a short visual history of western letterforms, starting with the cover of Nicolete Gray's *History of Lettering* which includes and illustrates everything from illuminated manuscripts to neon signs under the same heading – and few people are qualified to argue with her. Then the emphasis altered:

Against this historical background I outlined the two other aspects in terms relevant to psychologists in particular: a task analysis of the work of the scribe in any culture, and the interest in calligraphy in

Examples of expressive
calligraphy by Rachel
Yallop reproduced
from her book *Creative
Calligraphy*, Hodder
and Stoughton (1993).

the west, more in relation to the psychology of handwriting than in aesthetic terms.

At least I am qualified to discuss the first point as I was trained as a classical scribe in the years immediately following the second world war. My training had altered little from that of the mediaeval scriptorium, nor had the tasks that we undertook when the work of a scribe was still a viable craft. Our letters had to conform exactly to those of our master, as much of the work consisted of completing pages of memorial books. When I first heard Professor Kao presenting his work on the physiological changes of Chinese calligraphers when working, it explained for the first time my own experience of what I had termed coming out of a trance at the completion of a period of intense concentration on writing an extensive text. I even suggested to Professor Kao that he take notice of changes in body temperature as I usually 'awoke' shivering. There was one further thing that occurred at the moment of awakening, and that was a heightened perception, as if one were still physically attached to the trace that had just been produced. At that moment minute differences stand out clearly, whether sublime details or slight inaccuracies. A few minutes later such things can no longer be perceived, even by me, the writer.

Now, however, I would like to expand on this by analysing the task of the scribe. Although some of the components may differ between eastern and western calligraphy, the basic concentration demanded of the task remains the same.

What is the task, presuming that the scribe is sufficiently practised not to have to worry about the actual consistency of his letterforms?

1 *Spacing* Inter-letter, inter-word and above all line-endings.
2 *Practical problems* Inkflow and ink replenishment, necessitating altering pressure. Variations in the surface of skin or paper, or perhaps in the lines, if these have not been accurately ruled.
3 *Contextual worries* Including spelling or omitting or repeating words.

The intense concentration needed seems to require that the highly trained and practised function of producing consistent letters and retaining regularity must be unconscious. To write consciously, concentrating on perfecting letterforms can only invite inconsistencies and irregularities of spacing and pressure (here speaks the voice of experience, not the theoretician). The contextual aspects can then be the more conscious objective to control, within the personal discipline required to complete such a complex task.

These are aspects of the more disciplined and planned tasks of writing long texts. It cannot be denied that emotion can unconsciously be expressed by such writing – although too much emphasis on perfection and regularity can be instrumental in suppressing such emotion. It would be difficult to prove whether the effects on the body alter or if there is a different level of concentration when emotion is also being expressed through letters via the meaning of the word – more difficult in our writing system because a word, after all, is only representive of the sound values of the letters rather than the pictorial image suggested by a character. I know that Professor Kao has views even on the effects on the physiology of the writer when using different writing tools. My own years as a scribe and a teacher suggest that the attitudes of individual writers to their craft, or even to any particular task, would add even more variables to any investigation.

The recent interest in calligraphy in the western world can also be investigated from a psychological angle, rather than an aesthetic one, against a background of changed usage. The need for formal handwritten text has decreased until a once essential craft is more a leisure occupation. While accepting the therapeutic and pleasurable value of calligraphy, there is another side that can be interpreted more from the angle of the psychology of handwriting. Rather unkindly I would call that the affectation factor. Let us take the present fashion of adopting the renaissance italic hand as an everyday handwriting. Undoubtedly this graceful oval forward slanting hand comes naturally to many artistic individuals – architects, painters, designers, etc. Their hands move naturally in the way that is required to produce the strokes that make up these letterforms. For many others, though, this is not the case, and the forced and sometimes tortured letters that result betray the writer. The hope of improving self-image or public perception by adopting an historic style for everyday writing is questioned. Unless the particular forms come naturally, this indicates a desire to hide the true nature of the writer.

Another point: the effects of manipulating letters to produce an artifical effect is evident not only in the writing but also on the writer. Reports of RSI (repetitive strain injury) appear in some of the many calligraphic journals that are produced in various countries. 'Does your hand become numb while you practice calligraphy? Do you sometimes experience a tingling sensation in your fingers? Are you ever robbed of sleep because of severe pain in your arm?' This may be understandable in the case of an overworked examination candidate – but not really sensible in the case of an amateur calligrapher. It indicates, above all, tension. This could be caused by inappropriate strategies as is sometimes the case in everyday handwriting, but is more likely to be an indication of the tension involved in trying too appear what one is not. After all, our written trace is a reflection of ourself on paper.

Can I sum this up with the suggestion that it is our limited terminology that causes the same term 'calligraphy', derived from the Greek words for beautiful writing, to be used to express many degrees of emotion and many levels of function within the written trace. We must be aware of the dangers of generalisation in an area where personal as well as cultural attitudes differ so widely, while being open to the fascinating strategies involved in the passage of the image of a word in the mind transmitted via the hand to the paper – as a letter or character and sometimes much more.

As happens so often it is the discussions that arise that are so illuminating. In this case the greatest interest was from the Chinese in the audience, and also from those who picked up on the different attitudes to the word. One comment from a British participant left me unable to respond without being tactless in front of a distinguished audience. He reported that he was unable to comprehend the idea of expressing emotion through letterforms.

It is questions like this that make me realize how great the gulf is between those with an understanding of letters and those without, You can build an atmosphere of happiness, elegance or even vulgarity into a typeface, and this is a positive act taking a considerable amount of time to design and perfect. You do not have to be a graphologist to understand that handwriting is a reflection of the writer on paper and that in many circumstances attitudes to the recipient, or the contents of a letter, will be evident in the handwriting. Why then should it be so difficult to understand that calligraphy, whether formally written or informally, should not show emotion via the hand to the paper. Why should it be incomprehensible that the writer, in some circumstance, or in this case the scribe, should not consciously or unconsciously be affected by the meaning of the words that are being written, or the mood of a particular piece of work? Our alphabet may be less expressive than Chinese characters, and individual writers' own inhibitions may limit their capability to express their emotions, but in general, to those involved in letters their field is as creative as that of sculpture to sculptor. The form and line of a letter is as sensitive and expressive as the line quality in a drawing, and as individual as the intepretation of colour and light and shade are to a painter.

And where does this all leave me at the end of the day? As someone trained in the art of beautiful letters but not necessarily judging handwriting for its aesthetic qualities alone. As someone working in the science of handwriting and enjoying the analytical part of research into letterforms, using statistics to show the diversity of such forms and of the act of writing, but as someone valuing the solving of individual patients' problems more highly than the providing of evidence to validate my techniques. I am content with where my research has led me, and to have my work judged within this framework.

Epilogue

Whatever next?
Rosemary is one of the few who has faced the ancient and still unsolved conflict in handwriting between speed and legibility. In doing so she comes very close to pointing the way to the future.

In this book, calligraphy, guardian of clarity as well as beauty, is taken from its cradle in the manuscript and set to work among the hand drawn letters which underlie advertising, graphic display or just fun lettering in both a commercial and a leisure context. That is one road, but modern technology points also to a second. In another field, Rosemary has extracted from the work of a scribe its special expertise in letterforms and let it loose in the world of type design and computer-generated letters - to the astonishment and embarassment of many a professional technocrat.

More remarkable but less remarked is how her work relates to the structure of a script. The ancient scripts were made up of various forms of pictorial, ideographic and phonetic signs. Modern alphabetic scripts consist of signs only - until you look at numerals, punctuation or paragraphing, let alone road signs, and realise that the illustrative component has not gone away.

Today we write letters but read words. Anyone who reads letters in order to form words is not fully literate. The word, which we read in a single flash, is constructed out of letters which function as building blocks not unlike the elements which make up a Chinese character. Ligatures and short cuts erode the traditional outline of letters but produce a recognisable unit when read whole. There is a sense in which the written word is the modern hieroglyph. Rosemary calls it 'unconscious recognition'.

As with the word so with the sentence, the graphic unit which conveys an idea. We cannot yet tell where this train of thought may end, but the direction of movement is clear: towards a modern realisation of the most ancient principle of all, direct communication irrespective of language. It is an exciting time, and Rosemary is part of it.

JOHN SASSOON

References

Athenes S. and Guiard Y. (1991). Is the inverted posture really so bad for left-handers? *Development of Graphic Skills*, eds. Wann J., Wing A.M. and Sovik N., Academic Press, London.

Barnard T. (1979). *Handwriting Activities*. Ward Lock.

Brown F.M. (1985). Teaching English in an inner-city area. *Journal of the Forensic Science Society*, 25, 313-321.

Callewaert H. (1962). *Graphologie et Physiologie de l'Ecriture*. Nauwelaerts, Louvain.

Callewaert H. (1962). Physiologie de l'ecriture en ronde cursive. *Scalpel*, 42.

Callewaert H. (1963). For easy and legible handwriting. *New Horizons for Research in Handwriting*, ed. Herrick V.E., University of Wisconsin Press, Madison.

Eldridge M.A., Nimmo-Smith I., Wing A.M. and Totty R.N. (1984). The variability of selected features in cursive handwriting: Categorical measures. *Journal of the Forensic Science Society*, 24, 217-231.

Elliot J.M. and Connolly K.J. (1984). A classification of manipulative hand movements. *Developmental Medicine and Child Neurology*, 26, 283-296.

Fagg R. (1962) *Everyday Handwriting,*. Hodder and Stoughton

Franks J.E., Davis T.R., Totty R.N., Hardcastle R.A. and Grove D.M. (1985). Variability of stroke direction between left- and right-handers. *Journal of the Forensic Science Society*, 25, 353-370.

Gordon H. (19th. century, undated). *Handwriting and How to Teach it*. Marshall, London.

Gray N. (1986). *A History of Lettering*, Phaidon, Oxford.

Groff P.J. (1961). New speeds of handwriting. *Elementary English,* 38 564-565.

Hughes M. and McLellan D.L. (1985). Increased co-activation of the upper limb muscles in writer's cramp. *Journal of Neurology, Neurosurgery and Psychiatry* 48: 782-787.

Jacobson C. and Sperling L. (1976). Classification of the handgrip. *Journal of Occupational Medicine,* 18, 395-398.

Jacoby H.J. (1939). *Analysis of Handwriting.* Allen and Unwin, London.

Jarman C. (1979). *The Development of Handwriting Skills,* Basil Blackwell, Oxford.

Kao H.S.R., Lam P., Robinson L. and Yen N. (1989). Psychophysiological changes associated with Chinese calligraphy. *Computer Recognition and Human Production of Handwriting,* eds. Plamondon, Suen and Simner, World Scientific, Singapore.

Levy J., and Reid M. (1980) Variations in Cerebral Organisation as a Function of Handedness, Hand Posture in Writing, and Sex. *Journal of Experimental Psychology,* 107 119-144.

Lucas F. (1577). *Instruccion muy provechosa para aprender a escriver,* Toledo. Translated in Osley A.S. (1980) Scribes and Sources, Godine, Boston.

Mercator G. (1540). *Literarum Latinarum.* Translated by Osley A.S. (1980) Scribes and Sources, Godine Boston.

Montessori M. (1972). *The Discovery of the Child.* Translated by Costelloe, Ballantine Books, New York.

Otto W., Rarick G.L., Armstrong J. and Koepke M. (1966). Evaluation of a modified grip in handwriting. *Perceptual and Motor Skills,* 22, 310.

Richardson M. (1935). *Handwriting and Handwriting Patterns,* Hodder and Stoughton

Roman K.G. (1952). *Handwriting, A Key to Personality,* Pantheon Books New York.

Rubin N. and Henderson S. (1982). Two sides of the same coin; variations in teaching methods and failure to learn to write. *Special Education: Forward Trends,* volume 9, no.4 , Research supplement 17-24.

Sassoon R. (1982). *The Practical Guide to Calligraphy,* Thames and Hudson.

Sassoon R. (1983). *The Practical Guide to Children's Handwriting,* Thames and Hudson.

Sassoon R. and Briem G. SE (1984). *Teach Youself Handwriting,* Hodder and Stoughton.

Sassoon R. (1985). *The Practical Guide to Lettering,* Thames and Hudson.

Sassoon R. (1986). *Helping Your Handwriting ,* Thomas Nelson. New Edition (1994) Oxford University Press.

Sassoon R., Nimmo-Smith I. and Wing A.M. (1986). An analysis of children's penholds. *Graphonomics,* eds. Kao, van Galen and Hoosain, North Holland

Sassoon R. (1988). *Joins in Children's Handwriting and the Effects of Models and Teaching Methods.* Thesis submitted for the Degree of Doctor of Philosophy, Department of Typography and Graphic Communication, University of Reading.

Sassoon R., Wing A.M., and Nimmo-Smith I.(1989), Developing efficiency in cursive handwriting. *Computer Recognition and Human Production of Handwriting,* eds Plamondon, Suen and Simner, World Scientific, Singapore.

Sassoon R. (1990). *Handwriting; the Way to Teach it.* Stanley Thornes

Sassoon R. (1990). *Handwriting a New Perspective,* Stanley Thornes, Cheltenham.

Sassoon R. (1990) La Tenue de la Plume: Applications et Implications d'une Classification. *L'Ecriture: le Cerveau. l'Oeil et la Main,* eds. Sirat C, Irigoin J. and Poulle E., Brepols-Turnout

Sassoon R. (1990). Writers Cramp, *Visible Language,* volume 24, no.2: 198-213

Sassoon R. and Lovett P. (1992). *Creating Letterforms,* Thames and Hudson.

Sassoon R. (1993). *Computers and Typography,* Intellect, Oxford.

Saudek R. (1932). *What Your Handwriting Shows*, T. Werner Laurie, London.

Sheehy M.P. and Marsden C.D. (1982). Writer's Cramp-a Focal Dystonia. *Brain*, 105, 461–480.

Solly S. (1864). Clinical lectures on Scriveners Palsy, or the Paralysis of Writers. *The Lancet*, Dec.4th, 709–711.

Visible Language (1990). Ed. Sassoon. *The Hand and the Trace, Some Issues in Handwriting*. 24, 2.

Whalley J.I. (1969). *English Handwriting*. H.M.S.O. London.

Worthy W. (1954). *The Renaissance Handwriting Books*, Chatto and Windus.

Yallop R. (1993). *Creative Calligraphy*, Hodder and Stoughton.

Ziviani J. (1983). Qualitative changes in dynamic tripod grip between seven and fourteen years of age. *Developmental Medicine and Child Neurology*, 25, 778–782.

Index